# Trust is a Fool's Suicide

## By

## Lydia Ballard

## Introduction by P.K. Perkins

Visit my website at www.iamlovejoy.com

Facebook: Lydia Lovejoy

Instagram: @lydialovejoy

Twitter: @thelydialovejoy

P.K. Perkins at pkpjourneytosuccess.com

Printed in the United States of America

I would like to thank my brothers Antonio Ballard, and Michael Ballard for being my source of strength second only to God as a child. I wouldn't have had the will to survive if it wasn't for the both of you giving me the strength to keep going even when I felt like I couldn't.

I would like to thank PKP for believing in me and pushing me to complete this book as well as keeping me focused on my goals despite anything.

I want to thank my two beautiful children Neriah and Power for all that they are to me. Little motivators, time thiefs, my joys, my reasons, and my peace. You two taught me what true love feels like.

Lastly but most importantly,

ALL PRAISES BE TO GOD

# Table of Contents

# *Intro*

My left cheek burned and all I could do was look up at my mother like she was totally out of line for putting her hands on me … truthfully she was.. She wasn't my mother she was just the lady who birthed me and even then there were times that I felt she didn't do that. I loved to settle with the thought of being created and not birthed like the Adam of my eve…

The scent of 5 o clock liquor flooded our area of the foster homes visiting center from my mother's small frame …Her hounds tooth print outfit stood out as if she was begging for some type of attention that none of us needed. As if her high yellow complexion and long black hair wasn't enough.. Through all my hurt I looked over at my brothers

5

refusing to cry in front of her and be strong for them. I knew if they saw me break down then they would too and I wasn't ready to be anymore embarrassed then I already was. It was her fault we was here in this foster home in the first place with people that meant nothing to me. Five years old and getting visits from my mother like a prisoner; where was this suppose to happen and why did this have to be my life? I should have been at home watching lamb chops singing the song that never ends and being a kid like anybody else but this woman wanted to still do what she wanted instead of be the one thing any kid was suppose to have... The one thing that I shouldn't have had to ask for but was suppose to be given automatically; The first gift God grants every being that comes into this world. A mother... I'm young but I found myself asking God why couldn't he give me that? What was wrong with me already that I couldn't have the privilege of a mother let alone a real family like the Cosby's .. ? What did I do already to deserve this? Then god has the nerve to keep quiet as if he doesn't want to answer my questions, concerns, needs and prayers... As if he made a mistake and doesn't want to face me and own up to this. Not only did I have to deal with god and his neglect but also my mother and her addictive ways... There were numerous times I would find myself taking care of my two brothers and stepping over her limp body because she was high off the dope that her boyfriend, which was also my brother's father got her hooked on .. She would be so high; knocked out on the floor and he would begin looking at me in his high as if I was her because we looked so much alike... After a while I guess he wanted me like he wanted her ....He destroyed one life and now he was going to destroy mines too... I don't know how many times I stepped over my mother and wondered if that was going to be me one day ..then at the same time I would promise myself as life went on that I would never be what she was and instead be what she couldn't be because she had the devil on her back trying to steal her soul and also as her man destroying her body and mind...this devil killed, stole and destroyed just like they said he would. He made it hard for me to feel I was going to be anything more than what I was. Who does this to a child? Don't tell me I'm too young to understand because at the age of six I shouldn't have to. Where was the fire to help me identify with the hell I'm in?

# Chapter One

I couldn't have chosen a better night to carry out my mission. It was about eleven pm and the sky was dark and clear, the moon was full and bright glaring down on me. I swear people really acted differently during a full moon. I know I did. At that moment, the moon felt like my spotlight and it was my time to act.

His name was Andrew, a well tanned white man with muscles and deep blue eyes. It was something about those piercing blue eyes and that strong stance that turned me on like." I thought as I stood over his body admiring my work. What a waste I thought; men with his degree of handsomeness always put me in the mind of a prince charming. I blame Disney movies for my ideal perception of what a prince was supposed to look like. Never had I seen a black prince let alone king in any of their movies in my years of maturing so I guess Disney distorted my view of what a king was supposed to look like laid out in front of me. I watched the blood flow out of his neck which actually turned me on even more. I had just slashed it from ear to ear. "He deserved it. He will never be able to hurt anyone else again." I thought very proud of myself as I looked down at his private area that was also covered in blood staining my garage floor. It amazed me how easily I was able to take him out as I looked at the blank expression on his face. I knew that his face would be permanently implanted in my memory haunting my dreams but I felt it was worth it. He was actually rather attractive which puzzled me as I wondered why he did it. But I didn't give it another thought as I started to call E.

"Come take care of this." I said as soon as he picked up.

"Alright baby." He said calmly.

I hung up the phone and immediately started stripping my clothes off as I walked through the entry door taking me into my kitchen. My house was my sanctuary. It was the only thing I seemed to have total control over. I grabbed the remote off my dining room table and turned on some jazz music real low then went back to the kitchen and poured myself some White Merlot. I had a long day and it was definitely time to wine down so to speak.

I picked my clothes up and put them in my washer only to pause for a second to take a look at all the blood that had stained my new blouse. Just the sight of it put a damper on my night. I spent eighty dollars on that blouse. I pushed it in the washer with hope that it would come clean. I put on my favorite robe and took a deep breath in an attempt to remain focused.

I guzzled down the entire glass while listening to the sexy sounds of the saxophone as Little White Lies by Walter Donaldson played through my Beats by Dre surround sound speakers. The sound of the saxophone always seemed to calm me down after a stressful day. I was in need for some relaxation and a hot bath I thought. As soon as I finished my glass of wine I ran some bath water. Suddenly, I heard the garage lift up but I knew it was just E coming to get rid of the body. He walked in the house and just stared at me.

"You did a number on him. Are you okay?" He said staring into my eyes with that same look of guilt on his face that I've seen far too often.

"I'm good." I replied solemnly.

"Are you sure baby?" He asked obviously concerned.

I said I'm good.  I'm always good because I'm in total control. And he got what he deserved. Just get rid of him. Clean that blood up too. I need to take a bath." I said holding back every ounce of emotion as I headed back towards the bathroom stripping off my green satin robe to reveal my green lace boy shorts and a matching bra. I stood in my bathroom listening to the water run as I looked at myself in the mirror reminding myself I was serving a purpose and not just some sick twisted person. Andrew was scum that deserved way more than what I had gave him. He had just got probation for molesting a six year old little girl that I had to counsel into trying to be a normal little girl again. He was charged with rape but his money and high priced lawyers got his charges dropped down to reckless endangerment of a minor. The little girl he molested was his coked up neighbors daughter who was a single mother one step away from being a high end prostitute. I guess when he would go pay for her mother's services he would get her so high that she would be knocked out which gave him the window to reveal his sick self to her daughter. And knowing it happened to me before and how crazy I was, I wanted to at the very least "take care of the monster" for her as she so fearfully requested.

The killing and torturing didn't bother me though. I actually enjoyed relieving that stress. It was what I had to do beforehand, I thought as I stepped into the bathtub. The tedious task of locating John and getting him to notice me enough to ask me out was the hardest part. I analyzed every part of his behavior so I could learn exactly how to seduce him. That was the fun part. I feel like I was designed to conquer the mind. It was my super power. Your body is simply a reflection of your mind. You conquer one and it's nothing to conquer the other.

He asked me out at a local coffee shop that he frequented regularly every morning that I made sure he noticed me at during his usual time. I wore my long wavy shiny jet black hair down with a green headband. I had on little black workout shorts and a yellow and green tank top that had "Goal" across the front. I had the body of a goddess so in that workout fit that I knew made every curve standout, I was mesmerizing. My golden toned 34DD cup breasts sat perky with sweat glistening off them as I had just finished my morning run. I ordered a French vanilla latte and sat at a table right in front of him. As soon as he glanced up I stared at him so intensely with my brown eyes then flashed him a shy smile. I knew my super white post braces smile shining through my pink full lips implanted on my golden freckled face would be inviting to any man. I've been told that my freckles almost gave me an angelic childlike appearance so I knew it would definitely work on this pervert.

As soon as I flashed that smile and looked away innocently, he was intrigued. Men have always been sucker's for innocence. That is why men are so excited when they get a virgin. They want to be that one to takes away their innocence. Then once they've taken away her innocence they no longer care because now to them she's just like the rest... Dirty.

He came over to me as soon as he finished his cup of coffee and dropped off his business card.

"Hi, my name is Andrew Johnson and I think you are absolutely gorgeous, simply adorable. I would love to take you out to dinner some time."

"Nice to meet you Andrew, my name is Lilliana." I said smiling while taking his card.

"Would you like to go to dinner with me sometime Ms. Lillianna?"

"Sure. Tonight around eight would be fine with me. I'll give you a call." I said confidently.

"Oh… Okay…Sure that sounds great. I look forward to it." He said a little thrown back by my sudden confident demeanor.

"Please do." I said dismissing him with that same shy smile that drew his attention in the first place.

I continued sipping my latte as I watched him walk out the coffee shop. "Of course he would think I was adorable.

Freaking pervert." I thought in disdain as I downed my last drop of my latte then left to prepare for my date. He disgusted me. I just needed to get this over with was the only thing on my mind.

I called him and told him to meet me at this restaurant Andiamos downtown. I made a reservation under Lovejoy. He was confused as to why I had made the reservation when he was the one who asked me out. He actually seemed slightly irritated by it. I assured him that I was just being cautious seeing as though we had just met that day. He agreed although he wanted to pick me up but of course that wasn't happening either. I needed to be in control. And even more importantly, I needed him to feel powerless.

I showed up at the restaurant wearing this nice extremely form fitting dress with black thigh high boots with a tan trench coat over it. I had my long wavy hair flowing down my back rocking my signature black headband. I was rocking my signature burgundy lipstick.

"I'm definitely dressed to kill." I said as I looked at my reflection in the window pane of the restaurant and made sure there wasn't any lipstick on my teeth. I took off my sunglasses as I walked in towards the hostess to find my table.

"Good evening Miss…" The host said politely.

"Good evening Sir, I have a reservation under Lovejoy."

"Lovejoy? Yes, your party is already here." He said as he led me to my table.

"Hi, you made it. I was beginning to think you were standing me up." He said as he got up to pull out my chair for me to sit down.

"Oh, of course not. I've been looking forward to this all day. I said with a sly smile as I took my seat.

He was even cuter than I remembered with his piercing blue eyes and blond hair. He had on a nice gray Armani suit with a white button up underneath and a nice Italian shoe on his feet. I took note of his diamond cuff links as well.

"Oh have you? Well I'm glad I'm not the only one." He said confidently flashing his vibrant white smile.

The dinner went well and exactly as planned. I managed to slip something in to his drink when he wasn't looking and I could tell he was beginning to feel it. He couldn't stop talking about how mesmerizing I was and what all he wanted to do to me. I made sure to keep his wine glass full. I don't know what made guys think we wanted to hear about what all they wanted to do to us sexually on the first date. I mean if you're that comfortable then you should be able to talk about what all you want to do FOR her as opposed to what you want to do TO her. I just never understood that. Like we're going to say "Oh you want to hit it from the back while you pull my hair? Sure thing, stranger." The things they say after just meeting you and downing two drinks. Guy logic is crazy sometimes and they have the nerve to talk about women logic. Hmmph.

By the time we finished supper, he was threw. There was no way he could drive anywhere. I offered to take him home because I didn't want him driving drunk. He put up a fight as expected so I offered to take him to my place until he sobered up. I assured him I would drive him to his car as soon as he sobered up. This seemed to go well with him as he was expecting it would lead to sex.

As soon as valet brought my all black Jaguar XJ unlimited we were on our way to my house. He had no idea what was happening as he kept trying to rub on my thighs as I drove home.

"Put your seatbelt on." I said irritated as my car kept beeping letting me know that he wasn't wearing one.

"Yes ma'am. You like to be in control don't you?" Most people don't find that to be an attractive trait in a woman." He said laughing.

"Well clearly you're not like most people. Because you're standing at attention right now." I said looking down at his bulging package through his gray suit pants.

He chuckled rubbing his package. "Well normally, I go for shy innocent girls but there is just something about you Ms. Lovejoy." He slurred trying his hardest to focus on seeing just one of me.

"I'm sure there is. There's always been something about me Mr. Johnson. Tell me more about these shy innocent girls you usually go after." I said in disdain.

"Huh? What do you mean?" He said sounding guilty.

"You said you usually go after shy innocent girls. What makes them so appealing to you?" I said a little less confrontational this time.

"Oh yeah… well… nothing. They just seem easier to handle. You seem like you're going to be a handful." He said giving a weak laugh.

"You have no idea. Mr. Johnson." I said smiling.

I began to rub his leg as we were approaching my home. I needed to get him back in the mood and under the spell of seduction. Once under the spell of seduction, a man is completely vulnerable. It is their weakest state and they're willing to do   anything to make their greatest desires come to fruition. I kept rubbing his leg and his dick until I was twirling it in my hands. His eyes were rolling back into his head in ecstasy. As we pulled into the garage and I cut my car off. I hopped on top of him kissing him on his neck. He smelled so good. I wondered what kind of cologne that was. I loved a man that smelled good. That happened to be my kryptonite. I had to stick with the plan and not get too turned on. I think I might have a sex addiction because once I get turned on it's hard for me to stop until I get my release. I go crazy.

I ran my finger down his chiseled jaw and kissed his lips softly. If only he knew it was going to be his last kiss. I opened the door and exited the car on his side, pulling his hand as I got out, my heels clicking ludly on my garage floor. Once he was out I pushed him up against the car still kissing him. He was intoxicated not only with the wine but with desire as well. I leaned my pelvis into his very hard dick and held his face as I started kissing him more intensely. The sensation running down my spine was making me wet and weak might I add and not in a good way. His dick felt so inviting as I struggled with sticking to my plan. I started working my hand down his neck and chest as I unbuttoned it, softly moaning and nibbling on my way down. He didn't say a word. But his body said everything I already knew. Someone so addicted to power was completely powerless because I was making him feel wanted. And he was overcome with lust. Temptation is a motherfucker and ego is even worse I thought to myself as I started unbuckling his pants while he just kept looking at me. He couldn't say a word, he was in a trance. As soon as I pulled it out I also pulled a knife out the sleeve of my trench coat and he stumbled to his knees screaming in pain. The moment he got on his knees I stuck the knife to his neck in one motion slicing from ear to ear. He fell to the ground. And just like that it was all over. There was nothing quite like watching the life escape from a man who had no soul to begin with.

# Chapter 2

"That shower was everything!" I thought as I went to check on the garage. Everything was clean just as I asked. No one would ever guess what had just taken place less than an hour ago. I grabbed the wine bottle and went upstairs to my room to retire for the night. I picked up the journal as I climbed into my king sized bed and began to read the first page:

*I used to question why God brought me into this world. I tried to question my mom but that didn't really get me anywhere. She was always too high to understand me. It never seemed like she wanted me because she got rid of me every chance she had. One time she even gave me away to a lady she just met that very same day. It was late one winter night and I was a baby. I think I was seven months old. My mother had a male friend come over named Shock and he brought a friend of his named Anise. My mother and Shock then went upstairs and left Anise down there with me. Anise was like seventeen years old at the time and she was still in high school. I started crying really loud in my crib in the middle of the living room. Anise was sitting on the couch watching tv. She couldn't help but notice me crying so she yelled upstairs to my mother.*

*"Your baby is crying." She said. My mother never responded.*

*"Girl, your baby is crying." She yelled again.*

*My mother was in her own little world. She was upstairs with her friend Shock getting high off of crack. This was in 87' when the crack epidemic was growing rapidly. My mother was introduced to it by one of her boyfriends, Carl Haggartt. She became addicted quick and was on a downward spiral ever since. It completely changed her. My once sweet, confident, gorgeous mother turned into a rude, selfish, irresponsible monster when she was high off that stuff. She lost sight of everything that was important.*

*Anise grew tired of me crying and was a little worried that I had been crying for so long and my mother didn't once come down to check on me once. She went to the kitchen to try and get me some milk to drink. All the bottles were dirty and the kitchen was absolutely filthy. She cleaned out a bottle for me and made me some formula. She walked back into the living room picking me up and began feeding me. I immediately stopped crying. She noticed that my diaper was soaking wet. She found the diapers and wipes in a diaper bag by the couch and changed my diaper. I was so red down there like I had a rash that went untreated for such a long time. There wasn't any diaper rash cream in the diaper bag so she didn't know what to do. She called her mother.*

"Hey momma, what you doing?" She asked when her mother picked up the phone.

"Nothing girl just watching Jeopardy what you up to?" Her mother said.

"Well, I'm out with Shock over some girl's house and the girl has a baby over here with a really bad diaper rash. What do I do?" She asked her mother.

"Why are you asking me? Where is the child's mother?" Her mother asked thoroughly confused.

"Momma, I've been calling her for about an hour and she just hasn't come down yet or responded to me. I can't just let the baby cry." Anise said genuinely concerned.

"That sounds half bout crazy. Don't let nobody take advantage of you. You're nobody's babysitter." Her mother said irritated.

"Ma, just what should I do? The baby is as red as a tomato." Anise said worriedly.

*"That's what's wrong with these young parents they don't know what they're doing. Sure know how to make them but can't take care of them for shit." Anise's mom kept on ranting.*

*"Ma! What do I do?" Anise asked growing frustrated with her mother and her never ending mouth.*

*"Brown some flour child and put it on the baby's butt, that will take care of it in no time. You make sure you tell that girl that too because if she doesn't continue to do it then it's going to continue to get worse." Anise's mother said.*

*"Thanks ma, I knew you knew what to do." Anise said.*

*"Well yeah, I raised enough children on my own didn't I?" Her mother said bluntly*

*"Yeah, Yeah. Alright ma, I'll talk to you later." Anise said as she hung up the phone.*

*She then went in the kitchen to clean out a pan and brown some flour like her mother advised. She couldn't believe that my mother still hadn't come down to check on me. I was crying so loudly. She let the flour cool then she sprinkled the flour in my diaper and on my bottom. I immediately stopped crying. She held and rocked me close and I just looked at her and smiled. Anise looked into my eyes and was immediately drawn to me. She just had to come see me again.*

*When my mother and Shock finally came down I was fast asleep in Anise's arms.*

*"I see you met Shanna." My mother said in her slurred speech.*

*Her eyes were so glossy and she was so fidgety.*

*"Yes your daughter is beautiful. I wish I could just take her home with me." Anise said sweetly.*

*"Oh well you just name the day and you can take her whenever you want girl. I be needing a break from time to time." My mother said excitedly.*

*Anise was so shocked. After all, my mother had just met her that very day less than two hours ago. She knew that my diaper rash needed to be taken care of so she wondered if my mom would let her take me home that night.*

*"Well, can I take her home with me tonight?" Anise asked hopefully with a slight giggle.*

*"Sure girl. Just let me know where you live and leave me a number for when I want my baby back." My mother said laughing.*

*"Seriously??" Anise asked with surprise in her eyes.*

*"Yeah girl. You seem real nice. What's your name again?" My mother said curiously.*

*She didn't even know the girls name.*

*"My name is Anise." Anise said dumbfounded.*

*"Well Anise, my name is Diane. We're going to be good friends. Let me get her bag ready." She said as she got me ready to leave with a complete stranger.*

I closed the book and set it back on my nightstand. I was given this journal by the other psychologist in my practice, Maria. Maria was my best friend and the journal was written by one of her patients. She felt that by reading this journal it would help me deal with my own trauma that I went through as a child. I told her everything. Well almost everything. She had no clue what I did today or what I had been doing for quite some time now. All she knew was what was documented on my childhood psych report and the very little I remembered. She said that because I was in survival mode at such a young age that I learned to repress all the bad memories so I had the emotional and mental ability to break free from the situation I was in and be strong for my brothers. Maria was working with me to help recover those repressed memories. We met in college at Wayne State University. We remained friends all throughout getting our Master's and our Doctorate in

Psychology. I majored in Child Psychology and she majored in Adult Psychology.

As soon as we graduated we had saved enough money to open our own practice here in Troy, MI. Maria was the second person I ever told about my childhood well the little bit I could remember. She had figured I had to of been through something considering how crazy and fearless I was. She always knew how to make me laugh by making light of a situation, which was my favorite part about her. So when she suggested that it would be good therapy for me to read this book and eventually write my own to try to regain those repressed memories so I can finally heal. I had to admit it was good therapy reading this patient's journal but it still left me angry and confused. Watching the life drain from a child molester was even better therapy for me. And as expected that night when I closed my eyes for bed, his face haunted my dreams but it wasn't a nightmare. I found a great deal of peace knowing that he was dead and could no longer hurt anyone else.

# Chapter Three

I woke up to the sun blaring through my window as it began to rise over the Detroit River. It was such a beautiful scene. There is something about a large body of water that makes an environment feel so peaceful and serene. I was so thankful for everything I had and that despite everything I never lost sight of accomplishing my dreams. I absolutely loved my job. This is what I wanted to be ever since I was child. It's so rare that people actually have the same dream last from childhood to adulthood. Even more rare that they're able to accomplish it. I always wanted to help children who have been through something similar to what I've been through.

I had so much to do today. I had three appointments. One of which was a new child and that was always rough to get them to trust you and to open up during their first session with a psychologist. I couldn't blame them either. I was the same way as a child. I got up and turned on my music to get ready for my day. I hadn't checked my phone since yesterday prior to supper. I had seven missed calls. Four of which were from Khyail, Two from Maria, and one from my brother. I had three voicemails and I don't know why they did that when they know I don't check voicemails.

Khyail sent me a couple texts wondering what happened to me and why I hadn't called him all day. I actually felt bad because Sunday was our date day. We always spent that day together starting with church. We were going pretty steady now and we were definitely considering spending our life together. I loved him.

Everything about him. He was very protective and even

though I had no problem providing for my every need and

want. He always paid attention to everything I said and

would surprise me with random gifts and trips to places I

mentioned. But what I loved the most about him was that

he taught me new things and encouraged me and motivated

me like no other. It is so rare to find a man who is

comfortable with a woman's success and encourages her to

go for even more without it turning into a competition.

Khyail owned his own gym franchise, God Body Fitness

around Michigan, Atlanta, Miami, and Chicago. He started

off as a personal trainer then grew into an author,

entrepreneur, philanthropist, and renowned motivational

speaker. I smiled as I thought about how great of a guy he

was. I sure knew how to pick them. That's why he wasn't

intimidated by my success. He was equally as successful.

He is actually the one who keeps encouraging me to write the book that Maria wants me to do for therapy.

I quickly texted him to let him know that I was so overloaded with work yesterday and I would make sure to make it up to him tonight. I had no clue what I was going to do but I'm sure I would think of something. I finished my workout then showered, dressed and left for work. It was going to be a busy day.

I stopped to get Maria and I our favorite caramel macchiato from Starbucks to make up for not calling her back yesterday. I walked in and my first client was already there sitting in the lobby with her mother. I hate when my clients are here before me. It makes me feel irresponsible or something. I put the coffee on Maria's desk and mouthed "I love you" and went to my office. She rolled her eyes and mouthed "thank you" while on the phone. I went to my office and buzzed my secretary, Janay, to bring my new client back.

Just as I thought my new client, a little six year old girl named Stephanie, was very shy and withdrawn. It was definitely going to take awhile to get her to open up. It always took the new ones awhile to get used to me. She was an awkward looking little girl with two long pigtails and rosy cheeks on her golden brown skin. She was very well groomed and appeared to be very well taken care of. She was just incredibly shy. She reminded me of myself as a child. I spoke with her a little bit then I showed her all of the toys for her to play with while I had a word with her mother.

Her mother seemed as if she needed to be referred to a psychologist her damn self. . She wore a red pantsuit with some black heels and a black Chanel bag. She was tall and slender with long black hair. She was very aloof and rather fidgety. I'm thinking she was addicted to some kind of nerve pills. From what I gathered from her mother, Stephanie was referred by her counselor at school because she was displaying inappropriate behavior in class. Inappropriate touching and showing other kids her private parts was what the counselor wrote in her file. Her mother, Mrs. Reed, claimed she didn't know where she would get that from. That was a lie. That was another thing I was really good at. I believe the Christian folks call it the spirit of discernment. It was hard to get anything past me. I am an experienced and trained behavioral analyst. I could completely dissect a person's behavior within minutes of getting to know them. For instance, this lady had clear anxiety issues. She worried a lot about how others thought of her. I could tell this by her well maintained appearance and how she kept referring to the "nice job and home" she had. She was one of those types that believed as long as everything looked good on the outside then it didn't matter what was going on in the inside. I could tell this by her lack of concern about her daughter's behavior. She kept pushing me to recommend that she didn't need any further counseling. That was a red flag. And it meant that she was hiding something. My god mother used to always say that a fox smelled himself first. To me that meant that before other people noticed something wrong in your house, you're always going to know first. Whether you do something about it or hide it, well that speaks to your character and the type of person you are. I let her know that Stephanie would need to have at least ten weekly sessions before I was to make any type of decision. I then spoke with Stephanie to let her know that we would be talking next week and gave her a teddy bear to keep before showing the mother and child out my office. I always gave my new clients a teddy bear with my business card attached to it so they could reach me in case of emergencies. The mother obviously had an attitude as she stormed out the office mumbling and grumbling under her breath. It didn't faze me none. I was going to find out what she was hiding and for her sake she better not have anything to do with it. Lord knows I didn't need to add anyone else on my list.

Today was starting out crazy and I still had to figure out how I was going to make things up to Khyail. I had two more patients and then I was out of here. I was thinking about him the whole day. I never knew a love like this before and I didn't want to lose it. Although at times it felt inevitable. I don't trust people. You can't trust people. Trust is a fool's suicide. If I give you my heart and you break it, whose fault is it really? So I usually push people away when I feel their getting too close. But it seemed that despite how hard I pushed he always stood strong and never left. It was almost to the point where I stopped pushing and just let destiny run its course.

I decided to take him to Lucky Strike to play some arcade games. We were both very goofy and competitive and I knew he couldn't stay mad at me too long in that mood. I picked him up and held the door for him and everything. He thought I was the goofiest. I just couldn't help myself. I got a kick out of other people giving him the side eye when I held the door open for him. We had so much fun. I let him drive me home because I was buzzing hard and ready to devour my man. If nothing else would make it up to him I knew this would. I reached over from my passenger seat and unbuckled his pants.

"What you doing baby? You know I can't drive like that." He said.

"Just relax and keep your eyes on the road, you'll be surprised at what you can do if you just focus on what's important." I whispered bending down and placing my mouth on his dick. I loved the way it felt as it hardened in my mouth. I sucked up and down slowly at first with my tongue stroking that big vein at the bottom of his dick. I went all the way down to get the whole thing soaking wet and then I went to work. I started twirling my tongue around it as I sucked then stopping at the head and sucking firmly just on the head as his pre cum dripped in my mouth. That not only drove him insane but it drove me insane too. It was like when you get that first taste of something good and you just want more. I went crazy swirling my tongue around his head slowly then sucking up and down his hard chocolate dick ready to taste everything he had to offer me.

"Girl, you about to make me cum…." He moaned.

That only made me want more. I loved to hear him moan. And I loved to hear a man talk while fucking. Something about a man moaning that turned me on like no other.

"Just focus on the road and let it cum baby…" I whispered then slowly licked up and down his shaft before putting it back in my mouth.. He was jerking and moaning like crazy and I knew he couldn't take it anymore. So I got sloppy and wildly sucked as hard as I can looking up into his eyes while rubbing his balls then slowly licking and nibbling at his balls until he couldn't take anymore.

"I'm about to cum baby." He moaned.

I sucked on his dick tighter eager to taste my success. The car came to a stop and he jerked so hard. It taste amazing as I swallowed every drop. Luckily he was able to stop at the light right on time.

# *Chapter Four*

I woke up in his arms lying on his chest. That was my all time favorite place to sleep. I loved to hear his heartbeat synchronize with mine. It was the ultimate feeling of intimacy. I got up to go cook us breakfast and take my shower. I put the biscuits and bacon in the oven then went to get cute.

As I brought our breakfast to bed he was just waking up.

"You're the only one I know that wakes up this flawless." He said in admiration.

"Hahaha, thanks baby!" I said giggling.

To be honest. Steve Harvey taught me that. I think it was in his book "Straight Talk, No Chaser" but he said always wake up about thirty minutes before your man does so to make sure you're always looking good for him. I take my notes, but he didn't need to know all that. All he needed to know was that I woke up as the most gorgeous woman in HIS world.

We spent the whole day together. Working out, shopping, and then I took him to get us a couple's massage. We were having such a good relaxing day but I could tell something was bothering him. As we were sitting in the parking lot he was about to start the car but he all of a sudden just stopped.

"I need to know that you're serious and we're in this together." He blurted out.

"What do you mean? Why would you even ask that?" I said curiously.

"I mean, Lilly, you abruptly disappear for a whole day with no communication as if we don't normally talk every day. Your excuse is always so lack luster so it just leads me to question what this really is. That's all. You have to understand where I'm coming from."

The sad thing was I completely understood where he was coming from. I'm just not the type of person who is able to withhold emotion from someone I love, especially if I'm in their presence. If I had to do that then I would rather just not be in their presence. So sometimes I would rather leave then to hold back expressing my feelings to someone I love. It was hard to find the words to explain that to him without shedding light on my darkness so I was struggling to find a response. I went with the usual response of a girl in the wrong.

"Khyail, I'm sorry baby. I've just been hurt so much by different men that I just can't help but to push you away. Sometimes I just need a day to myself to reflect and realize that I am on the right track and you aren't that guy that's going to hurt me. And you know I love you. Sometimes I just need to unplug from the world. You know?"

I just gave a million excuses for one problem. Where they do that at?! I thought to myself as I watched to see if he was going to buy into my lie.

"Baby, I'm not that guy and I'll never be that guy to you. From the very first time you told me your story what did I say to you?

"That you just wanted to do everything in your power to erase my pain, to make it all better." I mumbled vulnerably.

"Yes and that's still true to this day. I love you Lilliana Lovejoy. Your spirit is beautiful in every way and you mean the world to me. There is nothing you can ever do to change that." He said as he leaned in for a kiss.

"I love you too." I said as I kissed him back wondering if he would still mean that if he ever found out what I had been up to these past months.

# Chapter Five

The urge to kill again was so strong. It was the strongest it had ever been and it felt like it was getting stronger with every kill. It gave me an unexplainable high and a release even greater than sex and I'm addicted to sex. But now my new relief was killing these men then coming home, putting on some sexy music and rubbing on my clit making myself cum as I was dripping off the power of literally having control over someone's life. But I also had to tell myself I was making a wrong situation right. I wasn't a bad person. I kept telling myself that hopefully it would take away th sick and twisted feeling I had in the pit of my stomach. I killed a total of three men so far. I had three left on my list. Everybody being in order and saving the best for last. He was the most important one on the list. Everyone else on the ist abused patients of mine but he hurt me. He started this shit. I owed everything I am to him and I was going to make sure he knew it. This cold, detached, cautious, and calculating person was awakened by him as I laid in the bed asleep. I used to be so sweet and trusting, then I woke up. I was lying in bed just thinking about what I remembered from my childhood and he was the only one I knew for sure hurt me. The other four men I had no clue and all I wanted was to find out who they were and kill them. As crazy as it sounds, I thought about that all my life; killing them. I wanted to take back my power that they stole from me or that I gave up because I was too weak to fight for it. I'm not weak any longer and I knew they couldn't take anything from me anymore definitely not without a fight. Eventually I would find out who they were. My foster care records were sealed tight as I tried numerous attempts to get more information but I was determined to get their names, addresses , and blood on my knife very soon. I looked on the nightstand and my attention was drawn to the journal on top of my bible. I picked up the journal as I began to read on the dog eared page where I had folded it over to mark where I left off a couple nights ago:

*I ended up staying with Anise for the entire weekend. She kept trying to call my mother but my mother never answered the phone.. She brought me back Sunday night because she had to go to school come Monday morning. My mother never gave her an excuse as to why she didn't answer the phone. She just thanked her and told her to let her know when she felt like watching me again. It became a regular thing for Anise to get me on the weekends. She became my god mother. And what an amazing selfless god mother she was. She was only seventeen and it was such an undertaking for someone her age to handle but she did it and she made it look effortless even with her still being in*

*highschool. Soon Anise's mother had begun to love me too.*

*I called both Anise and her mother "mommy" and*

*"momma" respectively.*

*My mother moved her boyfriend in the house with*

*her. His name was Carl Haggartt. He was a tall Indian*

*man with a reddish brown complexion and a long jet black*

*silky ponytail. He always wore a black leather motorcycle*

*jacket and black boots. I hated him. He was the same man*

*who got my mother hooked on crack. He was also my*

*father's best friend. Carl and my father used to deal heroin*

*together. They both got caught and my father took the wrap*

*for it because Carl had prior felonies and was older so he*

*would get tried as an adult and my dad would still get tried*

*as a minor. My father told and expected his best friend Carl*

*to take care of me and my mother and to make sure we*

*were good. You know, the usual request of a man to his best friend when he's about to be locked up for awhile. He took care of us all right, but, it was far from good.*

*Now my mother had a mouth on her. She could cut you into pieces with her tongue and make you feel about as small as an ant while doing so. Carl got my mother hooked on drugs so he could control her. He wanted to control her mouth, her body, her kids, and her life. Addiction is one of the strongest forms of control. What you make a habit becomes your life. And you will do anything to feed your habit and chase that high. My mother was a different person when she was high. What she used to do socially became an everyday all day thing. She seemed to always be high and when she wasn't high she was going crazy trying to get high. And the moment my mother went crazy and said the wrong thing to Carl he would beat her. He would beat her like a man in the street. It didn't matter that she was barely five feet and he was well over 6'5". He knocked her teeth out and replaced them back so many times I swear he* was a dentist. He always made sure she looked good whenever they went out in public. My mother was his trophy piece. She was one of the most beautiful women in Indianapolis. She was barely five feet. She had long wavy hair and she was the color of coffee with extra cream and she had a shape that women nowadays will pay for. He made sure she looked nice and he treated her like a queen in public. No one would ever be able to tell what happened behind those closed doors of the place we lived but hardly felt like a home.

One day my mother was sitting in the corner having withdrawals. One of the many side effects of addiction. She started begging for a piece of crack like a child in the candy store.

"Get on your knees Jill." He ordered.

She did still begging for a hit.

"Please baby. I need it so bad." My mother pleaded.

*"Actions speak louder than words. Show me what you're supposed to do when you get on your knees." He said.*

*My mother desperate for a hit crawled to him, whipped his dick out and started sucking it right in front of me, his five year old daughter Monica, and my two year old brother Michael. I was three almost four at the time. She was sitting on one corner of the couch I was in the middle. While she was sucking him off he reached over and put his hand under the Prince concert tshirt my ma had me wearing. My mother always had us roaming around the house wearing nothing but one of her shirts never any panties. He started playing with me down there. Viciously putting his finger in and out of me. I sat there fixated on the tv like nothing was even happening. Soul Train was on. I imagined I was there dancing down the soul train line with them instead of being there with him. He had been touching on me for so long now that I thought it was normal. I didn't see it as anything wrong. I had been watching him do it to*

*Monica, his own daughter so I just figured that this is just*

*what dad's do. All I knew was that it hurt. But shots hurt*

*too and they were supposed to be good for you, right? As a*

*child that's how I thought. And no one was there to tell me*

*or better yet show me I was wrong and he was wrong too.*

*After my mother finished, he reached in his pocket and*

*threw the rock at her. He then grabbed my arm so tight*

*giving me an Indian burn and dragged me to the bathroom*

*to endure his inner demon.*

*I always begged to go over Anise's house because it*

*was safe over there. I felt bad for leaving my brothers but I*

*hated being at home. It didn't matter what happened or*

*how many people called the police. Nothing ever happened*

*to him. It was like he was invincible. Everyone thought he*

*was the coolest guy ever. He always bought us the nicest*

*toys and when we went out we looked like the best dressed*

*family in Zooneyville projects. They knew he hit my momma*

sometimes but everybody blamed her because she had always been a fighter and always had a smart mouth on her. They looked at him like he was the one defending himself. Even Anise thought he was amazing. But she had no clue what he was doing to us. She saw that he seemed to treat us better than our own mother and we weren't even his kids. She looked at him like he was a saint or something. I didn't know what to do.

I told my mother that it hurt down there. My exact words were that "my kitty kat hurt." She looked at me and turned away. She didn't even acknowledge it. I was beginning to hate her. Here I was five years old and already hating my mother. I had a friend next door named Mimi and her mother treated her so well. She was so nice and caring and she was always telling her daughter that she loved her. I was jealous and I couldn't understand why my mother hated me so much. What about me made me so unlovable? By this time she had two sons with Carl and he *was just as horrible to them as he was to me. Carl was the sickest man I ever met and the sad thing was that I believed all men were that way. Carl would even bring his brother over some times to join in. I would long for the days that I would get to go over Anise's house. I would try my best to stay over there as long as possible even if I had to come up with a lie to get me to stay longer.*

*One time while at my mom's house, my daddy called from prison. Carl wasn't there. My mother was actually sober for once and talked to him for a little while. He must have said something to make her upset because she then gave me the phone going into the other room cussing up a storm. I loved talking to my daddy. He was the only man that truly loved me. He kept asking me how I was doing. I told him I was fine. I was lying. I wanted so badly to tell him the truth. But what if he ignored me like my mom did or didn't believe me?*

"Daddy, my kitty kat hurt." I told my daddy desperately.

"What baby? What you mean?" Tell your momma to wash it then." He said not understanding what I meant at all.

"No, it's clean. He just keeps hurting it." I said trying to tell him what was going on.

"He? What the fuck?! Who is he?" Somebody is touching you?!" My daddy said suddenly concerned with anger sounding like was going to jump through the phone.

"Momma's friend. He makes me call him daddy and he keeps hurting me." I said. I was relieved that someone was finally listening to me since my momma wouldn't.

"What the fuck?! Put your mother on the phone right now for me baby. It's going to be okay." My dad said into the phone furiously.

I gave my mother the phone. I don't know what he said to her but my mother went off on him then hung up the *phone. She slapped me and called me a lying bitch and went and sat on the couch like nothing ever happened. She then said you don't ever tell nobody what goes on in your house. That's your business not nobody else's. And after that she never answered the phone from my daddy again. Carl was becoming more and more invincible to me because even my own daddy couldn't help me.*

*Why can't we tell anybody what goes on in our home? Why should someone get the chance to continue raping you in private? Why should you have to quietly live in shame while he feels none for what he's done? I always wondered that whenever I heard someone say don't tell nobody what goes on in your house. And more than likely they didn't mean it in that sense but because my mom said it to me that day that's always how I took it.*

*Weeks passed and life continued as his power over us was constantly becoming apparent. I was so used to the pain, the bleeding, bruising, and walking funny the next morning after he snuck in my room. I didn't say anything and I didn't complain about the pain my underdeveloped vagina repeatedly endured night after night. He was only nice to me in public but once that door closed to my bedroom he became a monster talking to me like I was a sex slave made only for his pleasure. I knew so much at such a young age. How he liked it. What he liked. Every time I didn't do it exactly how he liked he would spank me. He often called me out my name referring to me as little bitch or hoe but it was baby girl in public. It would take everything in me not to roll my eyes when he called me that in public. He caught me one time and made sure he went so hard that I bled for a whole day. This was life. No one was going to save me so I had to deal with it until I was able to save myself.*

*However, one day my Aunt Olivia came over to see us and check on my mother. My mother and Olivia weren't as close as they should be because they grew up in different homes. My mother grew up with her Aunt Lola. Auntie Olivia was raised by their Aunt Viola and their other sister, my Aunt Sela was raised by a cousin. So they were all very different as they each grew up in different households after my grandmother died of Cirrhosis of the liver when my mom was just seven years old.*

*My mother was jealous of Olivia because she seemed to have everything she wanted. A nice house, a nice car, and whatever else she wanted. The aunt that took my Aunt Olivia in as their own was way better off then the aunt that took my mom in. My mother always felt that my Aunt Olivia rubbed her money in her face so she harbored lots of resentment. They could never stay in one room for long before they started going at each other's throats. My aunt noticed that I was dirty and threw an absolute fit as she drew me up some bath water and proceeded to give me a bath. But as she pulled down my panties she realized I was*

*bleeding down there and she started freaking out even
more.*

*"What happened Diane?! Shanna is bleeding in her
cootie cat." Aunt Olivia asked my mother.*

*"Is she? Well how should I know? Maybe she cut it or
something. You never know with that girl." My mother said
quickly sounding slightly nervous.*

*"Well, I'm about to take her to the hospital. Something
isn't right." Olivia said worried as she was already getting
me back dressed.*

*"You're not taking her anywhere. I'll take her if it's
that serious." My mother said jumping up from the couch
irritated with her sister.*

*"How is a five year old girl bleeding from her vagina
not serious? I'm taking her now Diane." Olivia said
putting my clothes back on and getting me ready to go.*

*My mother didn't say anything more after that. She just
sat back down on the couch and continued to drink her*

*beer. Olivia packed my brothers and I up and drove*

*straight to the emergency room.*

*After our emergency room visit it was found that all*

*three of us had been molested by my stepfather and his*

*brother. That same day before we even left the hospital,*

*Child Protective Services came to talk to my mother and my*

*mother acted as if she had no idea what was going on.*

*"What do I have to do to get my kids back? I'll do*

*anything." She asked the lady from CPS.*

*"Well Ms. Bowers, for one you need to get a restraining*

*order against Carl Haggartt. I know he has been beating*

*you but you keep going back to him every time. While he is*

*awaiting trial and out on bail I don't want him anywhere*

*near you or the children. Secondly, you need to get help for*

*your alcohol abuse. If you have a friend or family member*

*that the children can stay with until you finish this thirty*

*day program I would strongly advise you do so because*

*then and only then will you be able to get your kids back."*

*She told my mother sternly.*

*My mother agreed and we stayed with a family member for a month while my mother got herself together. After the thirty days, my brothers and I all went back home to live with our mother. Carl was gone but that was the only thing that was different. My mother was her same old self.*

# Chapter Six

Reading that was just what I needed to fuel my anger. I reached in the back of the book and pulled out my list.

4.) RONALD HEISER

I WAS READY. It was time for my next kill. The urge was unreal and reading that girl's journal only made me want to go that much harder in fighting for them. Ronald Heiser was the name of Hannah's stepdad. I met Hannah about two years ago she was literally my fourth patient. And her stepfather will be my fourth kill. She was seven when it started. The age I was when mine ended. I promised her that it would get better. Her father never went to jail. She seemed to lack even the teensiest bit of trust in adults when I first met her. I got her to open up to me. It was a long road though no doubt. It took over a year to get her to open up to me but I did it. She believed in me. I told her my story. I told her that I made my stepdad pay. And I told her that I would make hers pay as well. I met her when she was twelve and she is now fifteen. I vowed to make good on my promise. However, I just received word that Ronald Heiser moved to Brazil two years ago. And it looked like it was time for me to take a little trip. I called my clean-up man.

"Hey baby…" He answered on the first ring."

"Hey, we're going to Brazil. Call the family. Meet me there. You have two days." I barked.

"But….baby. You know that's not enough time to prepare for…"

"Prepare for what?! You don't do shit. I do this. I do what you should have done for me. You owe me. So use the damn account I set up in your name!!!! That's what it's there for. I expect you to be there in two days. I need to get this over with." I ordered into the phone interrupting him because I was perturbed by the audacity of him questioning me.

I hung up the phone leaving him no more room to rebuttal me. Dealing with other's incompliance is the absolutely worst thing about being the boss. Who did he think he was?

I'm passionate about my cause. A lot of people would consider me insane judging by my behavior as of lately and they might be right. But just think, they also thought Albert Einstein was insane and he was a fucking genius. I have good reason for my behavior and I could explain it very logically so how could I be insane? Just because it's not what society would consider the norm? Who are these people anyway that determine what's normal and what's not? According to society, normal is a rapist getting locked up for one to five years and a drug dealer getting locked up for life. That's your society and that's your system. Fuck society. Fuck normal.. Sometimes it just makes more sense to be crazy.

Because of my background in psychology, I knew that I was behaving irrationally but I couldn't stop. It's as if I was getting angrier and angrier by the day. I couldn't let go of the anger and resentment in my heart. Killing was the only thing that soothed me. This was something I felt that I had to do in order to heal.

It was imperative to me that I carried out this mission as soon as possible. There was no time better than now. I made a promise and I try to always keep my promises. I promised Hannah her dad would pay and he would.

So, Brazil it was. I thought of bringing Khyail with me. I believe I would be able to sneak away in time to do what I had to do and come back without him realizing what was up. And he had never been there before. He would love it. I had never surprised him with a trip after all the countless trips he surprised me with in the past three years. Brazil was such a beautiful place, I knew he would love it.

From my resource, I gathered that he had took up residence in Salvadore, Brazil which was a city that I knew very well. It was a historic old city, one of the oldest cities in the Americas as a matter of fact, it was filled with beautiful beaches and a lively culture. Definitely a good place to visit especially a good place to go with your man. I couldn't wait to surprise him. And I definitely couldn't wait to carry out my plan. I called Khyail to tell him to make sure he had the weekend off. He was questionable but he agreed to go wherever I would take him. I loved that about him, he trusted me.

I spent the next two days preparing for my kill. I listened to Hannah's therapy tape to get my mind right. I heard her describe in great detail the account of when he first began touching her. It always put me in a trance

71

making me think of my own hell I went through hoping I could just remember. She was seven years old when it started and it didn't end till she turned seventeen. I couldn't imagine enduring it for ten years with no form of relief. And he just got away scotch free then escaped to Brazil like he deserved a lifelong vacation instead of prison or better yet hell.

The plane ride there was rather long. Khyail took some pain pills and slept most of the way. He was kinda scared of flying. It was funny to me seeing a man who intimidated so many so scared of something that was so calming to me. Flying and swimming were the two things that seemed to scare him the most and those were two things that I loved the most. I loved being so close to the heavens and watching our land get smaller and smaller beneath us. And I loved to be surrounded by water. It provided me with such a feeling of peace and serenity. I'm a Taurus which is an Earth sign so I guess I just love every part of the world that

God created especially the things that man couldn't really destroy.

The first I wanted to do when I got off the plane was to go to the beach I thought as I sipped my wine and listened to my music on my ipod. I would watch the movie they were playing but flights always play something ridiculous that you never even heard of before. Like super low budget movies. You would think you would get better treatment in first class. As we approached our destination I couldn't help but to smile at him completely knocked out with his head rested on my shoulder.

We checked into our hotel room at around 3 o clock. I needed to leave as soon as we checked in. I needed to get this done and over with so I could spend some time with my man. I hadn't really come up with a full proof plan yet. It was time to do some scheming. I needed to meet with my clean-up man.

I met him at a local bar. He had already ordered me my cognac and he was sipping on hennessy and coke. I could tell by his facial expression that he was irritated about something but I wasn't in the right mind to care. I took out my notebook so we could go over the details and sat down beside him. I only drank cognac before a kill because it made me feel invincible.

"Hey baby." He said as I sat down.

"Please stop calling me that. Please just stick to your job. Now what is the plan?" I said feeling my irritation also begin to rise.

"You have to learn to let me in. I'm not going anywhere and nor is our relationship. So stop fighting it and just let it be. I need you and you need me." He said refusing to drop the issue.

"Listen! I don't need no fucking body. You hear me?! Nobody. You know how long I've been without anybody? All my life. So don't worry I got this. What makes you think that at the age of 28 that I finally need somebody? Especially you? What can you do for me that I haven't already done for myself? I built myself from the ground up again and again after life kept tearing me down. I did that. Not a mother, a father, a sister, a brother….not you. Just me. So what can you do for me? What can you give me? What can you be for me besides be my fucking clean up man? As a matter of fact I technically don't need you for that." I snapped angrily.

He sat there in silence dumbfounded by my words. I just couldn't deal with anybody telling me that I needed them. It irked my nerves. I needed somebody then. I don't need anybody now.

"Do you have a plan or not?" I asked as he sat there in an awkward silence.

"Not. Like you said you don't need me. You got this Lovejoy." He said quietly as he gulped his last sip and got up to walk away.

I rolled my eyes as he walked out the door. He was always so dramatic and emotional. For him to be so tough around everybody he always seemed to act like a bitch when he was around me. I knew it was going to be hard to handle it all alone but my pride wouldn't allow me to chase after him. He didn't chase after me.

I had to completely revamp the plan it needed to happen at a public place where I would be the last one they would expect. I was going to have to get close to him which again was the part I hated most. One of my connects told me he would be at this pool hall during the day lounging around as that's where he conducted most of his business there in Brazil. I decided I was going to pop up on him.

I pulled up to the little hole in the wall pool hall. I had on some ripped black jeans, a black crop top, and some combat boots. I didn't care how hot it was in Brazil, I always wore boots. You never know when you will have to stomp a bitch out and where else would I hold my spare gun? I walked into the building and it was super dark with dim lighting, definitely not somewhere I would be on any other occasion. It wasn't my type of place. I needed a certain ambiance that this place seriously lacked. I went straight to the bar and ordered my usual cognac straight. I noticed him playing pool with some other guys. I sipped my drink watching him intently. He didn't seem to have a care in the world. Just an old dirty man enjoying retirement. He was in his 40's, still rather fit, dark wavy hair, tanned skin, with a very nicely kept beard. He wasn't that bad on the eyes I thought as I downed my last sip and walked over to him hungry for the kill.

"Hey, can I play?" I asked coyly walking up to him and rubbing my finger down his chest..

"Sure Sugar Hips. You know how to play?" He asked smiling and winking at the guys he was with like he giving them a hint to bounce.

"I do a little bit. Haven't played since college though." I said innocently.

"Oh where did you go to school?" He asked as he proceeded to rack the balls.

"Not important. I'm not from here." I said matter of factly.

I continued playing pool with him mad that my cleanup man was somewhere acting like an emotional bitch. Trying to analyze this man's behavior was irritating me. He was simple to understand and I felt like I was wasting my time. This guy kept slurring his words and he reeked like cheap beer. Like that Colt 45 type beer. Crackhead beer is what I called it and that smell was the absolute worst to me. As he kept flirting and getting nervous whenever I played a long and flirted back I began to get more and more irritated. I can't stand a weak insecure grown ass man. Why can't you as a grown man handle a grown woman coming on to you? Do you no longer feel like you're in control because you realize that she isn't intimidated by you?  That's why these fucking pedophiles do the sick shit they do to these kids. They're too intimidated to engage in sex or even a meaningful conversation with a grown confident woman so they engage with someone that they far surpass mentally. It's pathetic that they can only find that in a child.  I was zoned out all bent over on the pool table contemplating what pocket to knock the eight ball in. I could kill him right now then shove this pool stick up his ass. It would give me great pleasure I thought to myself laughing on the inside. But this wasn't the place.  I wasn't prepared mentally. My emotions were currently out shining my logic. I needed to leave and get my mental back on track.

"I don't have all day" He slurred as he came behind me trying to grab a hold of my hips.

"You have as long as I say. Eight ball right corner pocket" I said as I knocked the ball in winning the game and gracefully swerving out of his grip.

"Damn baby, you didn't have to beat me like that. " He said with a nervous chuckle.

"Yeah I didn't have to. But you made it so easy for me to do." I said laughing.

"Yeah Yeah…" He said defeated. I could tell his ego was bruised a little by my win.

I told him I had to go because I had an important meeting to make. He gave me a flyer inviting me to some party he was throwing. Perfect location I thought as I took the flyer and walked out the door. As I got into my rental I had that weird feeling like I was being watched. I looked around and didn't see anything. Maybe it was just my guilty conscience catching up to me. I drove back to the hotel to go climb on top of my man so I could release some stress. Right now the sex addiction was stronger than the addiction to kill. Maybe it was the cognac but I needed to have a release or I was going to cheat on Khyail with one of these fine Brazilian men I seen on the beach.

I am very controlling when it comes to sex. Most guys liked it but some were a little turned off by me being so controlling. They were the ones who had problems with their ego. If he allowed me to be in control he would get the time of his life. I liked being in control of his nut. I liked being in control of my own. I liked feeling like I owned his dick and I made sure I did that every time. I liked to stay in control because I liked to control the experience. Guys are too quick to nut and focus too much solely on themselves. Sex is an experience not just an act. I don't have regular sex just like I don't smoke regular weed. It needs to be mind blowing or I'll take care of myself.

He was sitting on the edge of the bed watching ESPN as I walked in the room.

"Hey boo, Your fat ass wasn't playing. You already had food delivered before you got here. You're so damn greedy!" He said laughing.

I had already ordered room service to drop off what I wanted to eat but I ordered something extra special as a treat. I stripped down butt naked and took the whip cream bottle squeezing it onto my nipples. I looked at him intently then began sucking my own breasts cleaning the cream off of each nipple as I did so. The whip cream dripped down my little brown nipples that looked like little Hershey kisses sitting on top my perky DD breasts. He stared at me completely forgetting what was on Sportscenter. I squeezed some more cream on my breasts and walked over to him spreading his legs as I stood right between them. I gently lifted my breast to his mouth after sucking ever so softly on his neck. He licked all the cream off biting my nipples hard just the way I liked it. I squeezed some on his chest and started licking all the way down to his extra hard dick. Sucking hard and licking up and down the shaft that reminded me of a thick chocolate fudge bar… Stopping to occasionally suck down below leaving no stone unturned so to speak. He got louder as I switched back in forth sucking and licking between the two. I could tell he liked it by the way he moaned my name.

"Lay down baby." He said as he got up to slide in between me. He took the bottle of redi whip and squeezed the cream up my legs and all over my pussy as she dripped her own juices ready for some attention of her own. He slowly licked and kissed up and down each leg cleaning the cream off of me. My legs began to shake in ecstasy. When he got to my pussy he devoured it like it was his favorite peach cobbler. He slowly stuck his tongue deep inside of me then started flicking it so fast that his face was dripping my juices. He became insatiable as he flipped me over and started licking and fingering my ass. I was going crazy as he took a strawberry and slowly twirled it in my ass them began to eat it out of me. I came so hard you would think I was having a seizure. When I was finished I climbed on top and grinded up and down his dick real slow like I was riding a bull. The sweat dripped down his dark brown powerful skin while he gave into my power. As his moans got louder I began to bounce on his dick faster until he erupted inside of me. I fell asleep on top of him with his dick still hard inside of me. Thank god for birth control, I thought as I closed my eyes. I needed a nap.

Two hours later I awakened feeling refreshed and in a better state of mind. Sex always had a tendency to do that for me. It was about 8 PM. I woke up Khyail and told him to get ready. We were about to "party hearty" as my mom would say. We showed up to Club Ice looking like celebrities in all black everything. I had on a black t shirt dress that hugged every curve and gave the perfect view of cleavage and even my thigh as it slit up on the sides right under the crease of my perfectly round ass. The dress stopped in the middle of my thighs and my usual killer thigh high lace up peep toe boots adorned my golden shimmering legs. Khyail had on black jeans with a black

YSL tee and you could still see the crease off every muscle in his tshirt. Needless to say we looked damn good together. We were having a good time turning up in VIP with a few people I knew that E still managed to have give me a call once I landed. Khyail was mumbling something in my ear when I seem him walk past me on his way to the restroom. I downed my last sip of cognac and stood up to let Khyail know I was going to go check my makeup. He was in a zone drunk and just waved me off. I got up and smoothly walked into the restroom behind him locking the door as soon as I got in there. He didn't notice me come in as I sneaked up behind him grabbing his dick as he was holding onto it peeing.

"Wtf" He yelled.

"You know how I said you have as long as I say? Well your time is up." I calmly said as I sliced his dick in half. He screamed in pain and stumbled backwards against the urinal, blood splattering everywhere as his dick swung with blood. Suddenly he reached out grabbing my throat and pulling me towards him trying to grab the knife from my hands.

"You little bitch!" He yelled in pain.

I struggled to breathe as he had one hand gripped around my throat with my back towards him. I held on tight to the knife swinging it away from him scared for my own life. I knew I wasn't going to die like this. I had a purpose. I kicked backwards towards his private area where it laid split open kicking as hard as I can. He fell to his knees as I turned around to face him. I bent over and grabbed the top of his head and slit his throat then watched him fall as I swallowed the blood that gathered in my mouth from me biting my tongue when he choked me. My blood tasted nasty going down my throat but I couldn't spit it out. I couldn't leave any evidence, I was extremely cautious when it came to that. I stepped over him walking towards the mirror to gather myself. I looked a disheveled mess. I pulled the ponytail holder off my wrist and scooped my hair up into a messy bun then wiped the sweat off my face with a paper towel. I wiped his blood off my shoe and walked out the bathroom. I pulled the first fire alarm I saw which happened to be by the bathroom door and ran to Khyail as if I was the one scared. The entire club was in a panic fearing the worst. However, Khyail was actually calm, still drunk, but calm. The clubs in Brazil were always over packed way over capacity so people were fighting like crazy trying to get out. Khyail led me to the side entrance and we got outside safely, thankfully. I was actually pretty shook from the little fight with Ronald. It worked out in my favor per the norm but it still through me off guard.

To my surprise there was my cleanup man waiting in the driver's seat of our rental car. I couldn't believe he came. How did he know? I wondered. Khyail said what up to him and they exchanged pleasantries.

"Good thing you called him baby. Lord knows both of us were too drunk to drive." He whispered softly in my ear from the back seat like he was scared he would hear. My clean up man was the one person Khyail was comfortable with me being around. I looked at E smiled and said thank you. I had to give it to him he seemed to always be there when I needed him lately.

# Chapter 7

It gave me such a sense of relief knowing that when I told them it would be alright, I was absolutely confident that it would be alright. He would never hurt them again.

So many times people told me it would be alright just because they didn't have any other words to say. It was an empty promise simply meant to ease my mind for that moment. If only one time somebody would fight for me. If only just one time somebody would stand up for me and actually put a meaning behind those words. That's why I did it. I had to standup for them.

I was so happy to be home. Being on an airplane that long is absolute torture. I asked Khyail to go home because I just needed some me time. I had really fucked up the kill going off of shear emotion. I had to get it together. Despite how emotional of a woman I seemed to be, I always made decisions based off the philosophy, logic over emotion. So, for me to lose my cool both with E, my cleanup man and with that last kill was super reckless of me. I needed to get it together.

I was fresh out the shower curled up with a bottle of wine, my smooth jazz, and the little girl's journal. I just wanted to relax for the night and regroup tomorrow.

*I woke up to the smell of wood burning, smoke everywhere, and an extremely loud blaring alarm. I immediately started panicking, where were my brothers? I started running to the room where they were sleeping as I looked over at my mother who was too passed out from her high to even wake up to the screaming sound of the fire alarm. As I got to the room I was shocked to see my baby brother, Antonio's, crib on fire while my three year old* brother sat curled up in the corner with a box of matches in front of him. I was relieved to hear my baby brother crying loudly. I leaped over the pile of dirty clothes and grabbed my crying baby brother who was only four months at the time. I pulled Antwuan, my three year old brother's hand and rushed out the room and out the house to knock on the neighbor's door. Our neighbor was one of my mother's good friends well at least she used to be a while back. Now I think she was just her friend out of pity and to kind of look out for us. I didn't wait for her to answer the door. I sat Antwuan down on the mat in front of her door and laid Antonio down in his arms. I ran back in the house in a desperate attempt to wake up my mother. I started shaking my mother and smacking her face. She wasn't budging. I grabbed the house phone and dialed 911, a number I knew all too well.

*The operator got on the line and said, "911, what's your emergency?"*

*"The house is on fire" I screamed loudly trying to get my mother to hear through her drunken and high stupor.*

*"Where is your mother?" The operator asked way too calmly for me considering what I just told her.*

*"She's sleep and passed out" I got out before our neighbor, NeNe, grabbed the phone from me.*

*She got on the line and started explaining the situation like she didn't just walk through the door as if she actually knew what was going on. I tried smacking and shaking my mother again. She started waking up all groggily talking about "You know better than to wake me up Shanna. What the fuck is going on?"*

*She makes me so sick. I walked out the house to go grab*

*my brothers. I figured she would figure it out soon enough*

*right.*


*It seemed like it took the firemen forever to*

*pull up in front of our home but really from the time I woke*

*up to the time the fire truck came it had only been ten*

*minutes. The fire department, emergency department, and*

*police department were so used to responding to calls from*

*the Zooneyville Projects in Indianapolis, IN that they were*

*here in record time. They probably took bets on how fast*

*they could get here each time compared to the last time*

*they were here. They had to find some fun out of this mess*

*of a life we were all living in these project homes. We were*

*notorious. The police men were especially used to coming*

*through our door in particular.*

It didn't take long for the firemen to put out the fire. But afterwards they took my brothers and I on the fire truck to show us around. They gave us teddy bears dressed liked firemen and asked a bunch of questions like how the fire started? What was my mother doing? I looked at Antwuan to give him the look to not say anything but I knew he wouldn't. He wasn't much of a talker. I was still cuddling my baby brother close to me sitting in the truck with the fireman just rocking my baby brother. I said I didn't know what how the fire happened because we all woke up around the same time. The fireman then asked me, "Well, why did you call 911 and not your mother?"

"I don't know", I said simply.

I knew exactly what they were trying to do. The people did this every time some sort of emergency happened. They're always trying to drill us kids for information they *can use against our mother. I looked over at my mother. She was just sitting on the porch still in her nightgown smoking a cigarette looking a mess. I wondered when the firemen were going to leave. I mean the fire had been put out so they no longer served a purpose. Suddenly I saw a police car pull up with another gray car that looked very similar to a police car trailing not too far behind. I knew that wasn't good. They were probably going to put my mother in jail for the night and we would have to stay another night at Nene's house.*

*A white lady with light brown hair got out the gray car and walked over to us with a smile on her face.*

*"Hi, you must be Shanna" she said with this fake sweet voice.*

*"Who are you and why do you know my name" I said in my I think I'm grown voice.*

*She held her composure despite my response.*

*"My name is Ms. Kelly. They told me you had quite the mouth on you. Are you and your brother's okay?' she said without so much as a change in that fake sweetened facial expression.*

*This bitch clearly thought she knew me. This made me so uneasy. "One should never know more about you then you know about them." I used to hear my Godmomma, Sandra, say that all the time.*

*"We are just fine Ms. Kelly now why are you here?" I stated very rudely.*

*This time my rudeness seemed to get to her as her face changed slightly as she was obviously getting agitated. She seemed to be a little surprised by how advanced my conversational skills were at the age of five years old. That was more like it. I hate when people think they know you. I'm ten times better than anything anyone has ever told you about me. You have no idea.*

*"Well Miss Shanna, I am here to take you and your brothers to a nice little place for the night. Is that okay" she said in a slightly less sweet tone than she had been using before.*

*"Well sure Ms. Kelly, I don't want to sleep in our burned up apartment. Is my mother coming with us?" I said as I glanced over at my mother talking to the police. I was hoping she kept it cool and didn't start cussing out the police like she always did.*

"No honey, I just need to take you all for a while. You'll see her later." she said with the fake sweet tone.

"Oh, is she going to jail again" I asked already knowing the truth and not paying much attention to the her saying "a while instead of a night like she said before.

"I'm not really sure Shanna. Say bye bye to the firemen so we can get ready to go." She said all casually like we had all agreed that we were ready to go.

I looked over at NeNe sitting on her porch with her daughter, my bestfriend MeMe, as she talked to the other police officer. Oh Lord, she must be telling all of our business. Some people have to be a part of something even if it means selling out their friends, family and whoever else to do it. I mean I didn't really know what she was saying to *them I could only assume. But she was talking way too much to not be saying anything. I heard her say "I'm just so tired of dealing with this. She really needs help." That made me upset. She wasn't dealing with anything! We were! I glared at her and walked over to the car still carrying Antonio and holding Antwuan's hand. There was already an infant seat in the car. Check this bitch out! She just knew we were going to go with her. As if we had no choice in the matter. Apparently we didn't have a choice. Nobody was even trying to stop her.*

*Finally, my mother glanced our way as I was strapping Antonio into the car seat.*

*"Shanna what the fuck are you doing? Are you really about to leave with this bitch?" she yelled as if I really was the one making all the decisions. I didn't say anything. What was the point? If I said anything my mom would just*

*get even crazier and might try to hit me and she would be in way more trouble than she already was in. I just finished strapping him in and got in the car and closed the door. We had enough drama for one night.*

*"Look bitch, I'm not about to let you take my kids." My mother screamed as she attempted to run past the officer in her baby blue see through nightgown that barely came passed her butt towards the gray car.*

*I looked back as the officer grabbed my mother and slammed her against the police car. Her right 34 DD breast popping out as he pinned her against the car. The lady, Ms. Kelly, got in the car and drove away. We looked out the window as the police officer was shoving my mother into the back of the police car which was an all too familiar of a sight to see. I put the book down and closed my eyes as the tears continued to roll down my cheeks.*

# *Chapter Eight*

It was Monday so back to the grind. I called my secretary to see what was on the books for today.

"Hey, Ms. Lovejoy." Ashley said with excitement in her normal bubbly tone of voice.

"Hey Ashley, how many appointments do I have today?"

"Just 1, Stephanie at 2pm today. Other than that you're completely free. How was your trip? "

"It was good Ashley. Quick but good."

"That's good. I can't wait till I can take a trip to Brazil or better yet Jamaica and find me something super dark tall and handsome with a Jamaican accent and some dreads.

Ooh I can't wait!"

"I bet you can't." I said laughing.

Well I gotta go hun. See you around 1. I said cutting the conversation short.

I went for a run then came home to change and get ready for my appointment with Stephanie.

Stephanie and her mother were right on time at 2pm. Her mom was sitting on one end of the couch in her red dress with a black cardigan. She was still acting fidgety and nervous like she was hiding something. I was bound to find out soon enough what was going on. I hoped my intuitions were wrong. I took a deep breath and went over to greet them.

Hello little Miss Stephanie. How are you?

"Hi, I'm fine." She said shyly.

"Good to hear. And Mrs. Reed, I presume you're fine as well."

"I'm well. Just ready to get my day started and get this over with." She snapped at me.

"Well allow me to take her back then." I said abruptly cutting her rude ass off.

Stephanie grabbed my hand as I led her down the big cherry mahogany wood paneled hallway through my office to my counseling room. My counseling room just looked like a big play room. I told her to go play with whatever she wanted. I just waited to see what section she went to first. It was a tactic designed to get her to talk about what she ultimately wanted to talk about, which was what was bothering her. The whole room was designed that way. I remembered being in counseling and although I was scared to talk because you never know who you can trust, there was nothing I wanted more then to tell what was happening and have my secret in safe hands that would hopefully save me from this hell.

As I expected she went to the doll house. I watched her grab the little girl and play with her for a moment. I just sat there on the sofa beside the dollhouse just watching her yet making it seem as if I was preoccupied on the phone so she could continue playing how she normally would. I watched her grab the mother and use the mother to beat on the little girl doll saying liar as she did. That corresponded with the report the teacher sent over in regards to how she played at school. She then grabbed the father and made him get on top of the little girl right after the mother doll beat her. I wasn't surprised. It was consistent with everything her school officials were saying.

Typically my patients opened up about their abuse in various forms of play. I had several different forms that I used but the dollhouse was the most commonly used with the girls. I had action figures for the boys, I had boy and girl cabbage patch dolls, and then good old fashioned coloring that seemed to be popular among both sexes. I sat there watching her play she seemed to get bored with that and started playing with the baby doll holding her close and stroking her hair as she rocked back and forth in the rocking chair..

"Are you okay?" I asked gently.

She nodded her head yes.

I asked her if she knew why she was here.

"My teachers told my mom that something was wrong with me." Stephanie said.

She told you that? I asked getting more and more irritated with her mother.

She nodded yes again.

"Oh honey there is nothing wrong with you." I said rubbing her hand. I wanted to hug her real tight and let her know it would be okay. I had already decided.

We just think there might be some things going on in your home that shouldn't be. What do you think?" I prodded further.

She shrugged her shoulders up and down.

"Do you want to talk about it?" I asked gently.

She shrugged her shoulders again.

"I noticed you playing with the dollhouse. Does your mom hit you like that at home?"

"Sometimes." She said looking away innocently."

"What about your stepdad does he do that to you too?"

"Yes."

"Does he do anything else to you?" I kept going since she was willing to talk.

She nodded her head again.

"Do you want to talk about it?" I asked.

"Yes, but I'm scared."

"I know Stephanie. I want you to trust me. I'm here to help you and I can assure you I can stop whatever is scaring you."

"You promise?" She asked timidly.

"I promise." I said confidently.

It normally took my clients a couple visits before they start opening up the way she did but it took only one session for Stephanie. It was something about her energy. It seemed to align heavily with mine. You know how you meet someone and you just click really well together. She was drawn to me and surprisingly I was really drawn to her too.

# Chapter 9

I called E.

"What up baby." He answered on the first ring.

"Hey man. Let's meet at our spot.  We need to talk." I blurted into the phone.

"Sure thing baby. You talking now?"

Yeah, right now. I'm putting my clothes on as we speak." I said then hung up the phone without giving him a chance to get another word in.

I threw on some yoga pants and a t shirt and got my bag ready to head out the door.  I met E at the gym.  E had been training me how to fight for a minute now.  He was a black belt in Hapkido martial arts and I loved sparring with him. Hapkido is a martial art in which you use your opponents energy against them. Everything you are is the sum of your energy which is why I was so intrigued by this form of martial art. We threw some bows and talked about the next kill.

So who's next? " He asked curious to know my next target.

I kept the list under tight wraps because I knew he just wanted to get shit over with so he could stop worrying about me. He would probably take the list and handle them all in no time. This was more so therapy for me. Stress relief I guess. I loved the feeling of watching the life escape from a soulless man. My list was dwindling down though. After him there was only one more person on the list before my main guy. A part of me wasn't ready to stop any time soon. And the justice system fucks up. I only kill the ones who got away with it, the ones where the justice system failed the victim. No way should a guy get anything less than life for rape. They need to all be in their own jail raping each other for the rest of their life. But until that was reality I felt like my service was needed. I wasn't ready to stop at all.

"There's this new patient of mine. Her stepdad is abusing her. The only thing is that I want to take care of both her parents because they're both horrible because her mother knows about it. But then she'll be an orphan. We'll literally be leaving this girl with no family. But you should have seen her face as she was telling me what they did to her, she was so scared." I said.

"She's better off without him then right?" said E.

"Yeah but how much better off is she as a child of the system? This system can't protect anybody. So in reality I don't know what to do." I said feeling defeated.

"You know what to do baby. Handle your business. You always come up with something."

"I don't know yet. There's only one more person aside from then you know who."

"Damn you ready to handle that now?" He said all excited. "That means you're done right?" He asked with hope in his eyes.

He felt I was playing a dangerous game and that I thought I was invincible. I feel that I'm often in the midst of a dangerous game and I always come out on top. Honestly, I felt invincible. I overcame everything I been through. And plus I was ridding the world of disgusting horrid people how could the Universe not rock with me?

"I don't know. I don't want to be. Truth be told this shit feels good as hell. I feel like I'm doing a service to the community." I laughed to him jokingly but still very serious.

We finished training then went over final details and I told him I would send them to his email later today while at work. I gave him a kiss on the cheek and grabbed my bag and walked out the gym. I went home to read more of her journal:

*I remember that all I could think about as we were pulling away was if I was ever going to see my mother again. As much as I felt like I hated her all I really wanted was to feel her love. There was nothing I wanted more than to feel loved by her. I never felt it from her. She always seemed to be too high to pay attention to me let alone care for me. It felt like there was always something more important. If it wasn't that devil of a man that she was with then it was that white devil she was inhaling through that glass pipe. She was always choosing something over me.*

*We pulled up to a large brick house that looked more like the the Beast's mansion from Beauty and the Beast. The lady helped us all out the car and we went through the double doors. When we walked in we were met by a large dark hallway. I noticed there were rooms all down the hallway. We walked into what I assume was the office and she told us to sit down on the couch while she sat at a desk and talked to the manager of the group home. They talked for maybe thirty minutes and signed a whole bunch of paperwork. After that we went down the very end of the hallway where we were led to a very large room about the size of a gym that was filled with kids. There were like sixteen kids in the room all different ages. There were toys, bookshelves and different play stations where you could choose what you wanted to play. It actually seemed pretty fun.*

*We were in that room for what seemed like hours before they led us to another room, this room was a bedroom with two beds. They tried to take the baby away from me but that wasn't happening. Not only was I not letting that happen but he wasn't letting that happen either. Antonio was only one years old but to him I was the only mother he had. Antonio was born addicted to crack cocaine. By the time he* got here my mother was so addicted to crack herself that there was hardly ever a moment when she was sober, especially when she had a man that was constantly providing her all the access to her habit to ensure that she was too high to care about what he was doing to her children. I took care of Antonio ninety nine percent of the time and yes I did this at the tender age of five. So when I say that Antonio would go crazy whenever they tried to take him away from me I mean he would go stone cold crazy. He would throw a fit, crying all while beating his head on the floor. So they had no choice but to bring a crib in my room for him. Antuan went to a room with some other boys that were in the group home and Antonio and I had a room to ourselves.

I loved that little boy like he was my own child. I had no concept of how a five year old was supposed to act. I felt grown. I mean I had already been through so much in my five years that you couldn't tell me I wasn't grown. I had

*men messing with me like I was a grown woman. There*
*really wasn't anybody who could tell me that I wasn't*
*grown at that point in my life. So to me I was his mother*
*and he was my child, he even called me momma. And I*
*would protect him as if I birthed him.*

*That one night that she said we would go away for*
*"awhile" turned into days. Those days turned into weeks. I*
*felt so alone.*

*Three weeks later, my mother finally came to visit. We*
*met in the visiting room. It was a smaller version of that*
*large community playroom that all the kids were in. There*
*was a security guard at the door. My brothers and I were*
*seated at a couch waiting for her to come in. She had on a*
*houndstooth print suit. I'll never forget that because she*
*looked so classy, beautiful and sophisticated. I had never*
*ever seen her like that. Her hair was long and wavy down*
*to the middle of her back. She had on her normal red*
*lipstick and that suit was fitting every curve of her body.*

*She was gorgeous. The security guard couldn't stop staring and she only intensified his stares because she kept flirting with him. She had a Barbie doll and two hot wheel cars in her hand to give to us. It was a Hawaiian Barbie doll. I remember being so happy.*

*That happiness was short lived because the moment she got close I smelled the alcohol on her breath. I became so angry.*

*"Hey baby girl, mommas here." She slurred.*

*"You're not my momma." I yelled.*

*I was so angry. When I first saw her I was under the impression that she had went to rehab and got herself together and we were all going home with her. I thought she was coming to take us away from these strangers but after smelling that liquid devil on her tongue, I knew it was only a matter of time before she showed that devil.*

*"I am your momma. You came out of my pussy. I brought you into this world and I'll take you out." She said as she slapped me right across my face.*

*The security guard immediately came to grab her and she was fighting and cussing like a mad woman.*

*"You ungrateful little whore. He gave you everything you ever wanted and you fucked it up for me with your big mouth. You ruined everything. And now you're here with our baby boys and these people you don't even know. He won't even come see me no more and it's all your fault." She screamed.*

*I wasn't battling with what I felt for her any longer. I now knew that I hated her. I didn't care if I ever seen her again. She was scum beneath my toes. I got that from the little rascals but it was so fitting. I gave her a blank stare. She needed to know that I didn't care and her words did nothing to me.*

*She switched it up.*

"Baby, I'm sorry. I didn't mean too. You know I love you. You're my sweet baby." She said softly and sincerely.

My mother was battling a strong demon and it was very rare for her to ever be on the winning side. In hindsight, I think she was bipolar. She would go from sweet to mean in a matter of minutes.

I didn't say anything and I didn't cry. My time for crying was over. I had to be strong for my brothers. We were all we had. I faced the harsh reality that at the age of five I was really alone. It was all about survival from this moment on. At that point I would have rather of been in the group home as an orphan with these complete strangers then at home with my mom. At least I was safe there. Sometimes complete strangers will treat you better than your own flesh and blood. That's what I learned from her first and last visit.

# *Chapter Ten*

Stephanie's first session already had me adding them to the list. But where would that leave Stephanie? I had such negative memories of being in foster care I couldn't imagine putting another child there. But she's getting molested you say? She'll get molested there is what I say, I had to come up with a better plan. I know for one thing I was definitely going to be keeping a watchful eye on her mom and stepdad and I was going to find out exactly what was going on. But first I had to deal with the next person on my list and then I'll decide from there what to do about Stephanie.

Brian Waverly, he was the next person on my list. He had pretty much the same story as all the rest. One of my patients had been molested by him. And my patient, Chris was only thirteen years old when it happened. He was raped by his football coach. It went to trial and he was found not guilty. This was the third time he was charged with a crime like this and found not guilty. I didn't understand it. I would sit in the courtroom all the way in the back row but every time he turned around and I seen that evil smug smile, I knew he was guilty. I believed my patient and I knew he needed justice to be served on his behalf in order for him to properly heal. I planned on being that swift justice. I had E following him for awhile now and there were a couple places we could do the job. I wasn't really feeling the going out on a date with them routine anymore. It was far too difficult for me to contain my disgust long enough to sit through an intimate conversation with them. So it was either going to be handled at his gym, his job or his home. He didn't really go anywhere else. Being that he worked for the Detroit Police Department as a detective in the homicide division his job became immediately out of the question. It was so risky going after him period because of his job position however; I was feeling very risky as of late. I was getting bored with how I was currently handling things. It all happened to quick. I didn't get any time to do what I really wanted to do. There was no real torture and sometimes I don't even think the pedophiles understood why I was killing them. What's the point of punshing people if they don't know what they'e being punished for? This time was going to be different. I think about how long the abuse was going on with my patient Chris it was a total of three years until he turned sixteen. Surely I can make their pain last longer than thirty seconds. Death was far too kind of a punishment for their devious abhorrent behavior. So with how I was feeling now I wanted to do it at his gym which coincidently was one of the gyms Khyail owned. This was going to take a serious plan to undertake everything that came with killing this piece of shit, an accomplished Detroit Police Officer. It might be best for E to come up with this one as long as he gave me my three days to torture him.

*We were in the group home for maybe three months before a family came and wanted us to be their foster kids. I had made it very clear from the beginning that there was no way that they were separating us. My brothers were all I had and there was no way that I was going to lose them too. So they knew that if they wanted any one of us then they were to take all of us.*

*The first family that I can remember was the white family. We had been to three houses prior to that but we weren't there long so I can't remember them.*

*This was the biggest house I've ever seen in my life. They lived on a farm. It was a ton of acres. I don't know how many, I just know it was a lot. It was a beautiful big red brick house. There was a barn in the back with a stable that held two beautiful horses. A white horse named Lightning and a black horse named Thunder. They were absolutely beautiful and it was my first time ever seeing a horse. There were other farm animals too but the horses were the only animals that interest me. There was also a big pool in the backyard with a slide. From the outside looking in it would seem as if we caught the jackpot with this foster family.*

*Of course I should've known better. If it looks too good to be true, it usually is. They had two daughters of their own and two foster daughters who just so happened to be African American. One girl was fifteen and her sister was eight. They put us in the bedroom with them. Their names were Mya and Melany. The oldest, Melany seemed to be so different, rude, and creepy but only to me. She was really nice to my brothers and I think she was scared of their real daughters.*

*Their real daughters were the evil step sisters straight out of a Cinderella story. They would do the most horrible things to us. For instance, one time they made me come down the slide into the pool promising that they would catch me. I remember crying so hard because in my mind I knew they weren't going to catch us. The one sister climbed me up the ladder as I was crying and begging her not to and the other promised to catch me. She pushed me down the slide and I was under water for what felt like forever before she finally saved me. That day I vowed to learn how to swim. It feels like you're losing control over everything when you're drowning and losing control over your life is the worst feeling ever. But that's not all they did, they would put our heads into the snake holes or soak the chips in pool water and then give us the bag and force us to eat the entire bag of soggy chips. There was absolutely no end to them. It was as if every day they thought of new ways to torture us.*

The mother was more mild mannered but she was still rather mean. They kept us all in one room and made us clean up the house all day. For each and every meal they fed us peanut butter and jelly sandwiches. Occasionally they would give us cookies with the milk to go along with it. One time I asked for a little bit of what they were eating.

"Sure girl, you can have a little bit." She said as she smirked.

She then put three threads of chicken on my plate, three grains of rice, and three peas. Her and her two daughters erupted in laughter and Mya just looked at me rolled her eyes and shook her head in disgust as if she was ashamed that I even asked.. I realized where her daughters got their evil attitude from.

The father was a different story. He seemed very nice. He was hardly ever there to begin with. And when he was there he seemed pretty nice and he always would scold his own daughters on how they treated us. Mya loved when he

125

*was home. I just didn't get it because her usual attitude that she had went away.*

*He seemed to be a pretty good guy. He taught me how to ride a horse. He put me on top of Lightning, the white horse and got behind me while he taught me. Whenever I saw him on that horse he reminded me of a Disney Prince. He was tall, white with dark silky hair. He looked just like the princes in all the fairytale movies to me. Why weren't there any black princes? For those first couple of weeks he was completely changing my view on men. Or white men I should say. He was so nice and he always brought us things when he came home from trips. In my mind I had decided that black men were evil and white men were nicer.*

*One night he came into our room. I was asleep on my bottom bunk and my brother was on the top bunk. Mya was on the bottom of the other bunk bed with her sister on the top of that bunk bed. He sat on Mya's bunk bed and started playing in her hair. Mya smiled. They thought we were*

*asleep.*

*"Daddy missed you baby girl." He said still stroking*

*her hair.*

*"I missed you too daddy." She said.*

*"Can you show me how much you missed me baby*

*girl?"*

*"Yes daddy." She said as she got off the bed and*

*started unbuckling his pants.*

*I couldn't believe it. It was almost the same thing I*

*heard my stepdad say to my mother although he said it way*

*meaner than that.*


*I absolutely couldn't believe what was happening right*

*before my eyes. It was as if she was actually enjoying what*

*she was doing to him. She was moaning and just way to*

*into it and he was playing in her hair. After she finished*

*with him, he bent her over the bed and went in her from*

*behind. Again she was all into it. He was going so slow and being so gentle. It was nothing like what my step dad would do. He finished and gave her a kiss and said, "Thank you, Princess. You always treat me right.*

*As he was pulling up his pants he noticed that I was watching.*

*"Look who's up." He said with a smile.*

*I quickly closed my eyes as if I wasn't already caught. He came closer. He started rubbing my hair the same way he was rubbing hers. I was so scared.*

*"Did you like what you saw?" He said gently.*

*I shook my head no.*

*"She's not ready yet Daddy." Mya said abruptly. "She's going to react the same way Melany did when we tried it with her." She said with an attitude.*

*Now I couldn't believe what I was hearing. How could she have let him do anything like that to her sister. She was pure evil to me.*

*"No, I don't believe that. She's not new to this. She's been going through this longer than you actually." He said matter of fact.*

*They were speaking about me in front of me as if I wasn't there. And how did he know what I had been through before. What type of place was this?*

*He then told me that he wouldn't be so rough.*

*Men like me are gentler. We know exactly how to treat a woman and how to make you feel just as good as you will make me feel." He said as if he was somehow any less of a creep than what my stepdad was because he was white.*

*He then called Mya over to "make me feel good." She acted like she had an attitude but she came over anyway. She then began to lift up my nightgown and lick me down there. At first I was pushing her away but he held my hands down. It then started to feel good. It was a completely different feeling then I've ever felt before. It lasted for about five minutes and afterwards he put his finger inside*

129

*of me twirled it around a lot and then pulled it out and stuck it in my mouth.*

*"You're definitely ready." He said.*

*I didn't know what to feel from that point. Why did it feel good? What did that say about me?*

*From then on he proved to me just how ready I was. Almost every other night he came in there and made us both "feel good" as he called it. He was also making us do things to each other that I never knew even existed. And the absolute worst part was I would take this any day over what my stepdad did to me. And he was right, it did feel better. It still felt wrong but at least it didn't hurt.*

*At this point I was six years old in the first grade. I was becoming pretty use to the routine and I was okay with it because it was better than being at home with my mom and the random people she let in the house. I had no clue that there was something better out there for me. I was okay with the peanut butter and jelly sandwiches and I was okay with the evil daughters, and I was actually okay with him*

*coming in regularly to make me "feel good" as he would*

*put it.*

*However, what I wasn't okay with was having anybody*

*messing with my brothers. And that was exactly what*

*happened that became the straw to break the camel's back.*

*One day I woke up in the middle of the night to find*

*Mya feeling on my middle brother, Antuan. She had his*

*underwear down and was playing with it and kissing him*

*all over. I completely lost it. I started attacking her and*

*yelling and screaming till everyone woke up. The lady*

*came into the room and I told her what Mya was doing. I*

*was going crazy. And I wanted to kill Mya. The next day all*

*three of us were returned back to the orphanage as if we*

*were toys that were tried out and then returned as if we*

*came broken or something.*

I drifted off to sleep as the book fell out my hands onto
my lavender sheets.

# Chapter Eleven

Today was the day! E came up with a full proof plan
and we were carrying it out today. Good thing, because I
was getting antsy ready to get this good stress relief in.
Every time I read a section of that girl's journal I would get
a weird energy over me that I simply could not explain. It
was as if I would envision myself in the little girl's place as
I read her words. It made me furious. I thought of my own
past and how I couldn't remember much of anything. Just
what was on the case report which said I was molested by
four different people since I was three years old. Can you
imagine knowing something so terrible happened to you
but not remembering anything completely? Can you

imagine having flashbacks of men doing horrible things to you, knowing it was done but having absolutely no real recollection of the events occurred? I wanted nothing more than to know exactly what had happened to me. Truth be told if I knew who those four men were then I would be finding and killing them. My patient's attackers were just surrogates for my own. I closed her journal and began to get ready for my day.

Despite how risky it was I met up at Perk's gym to workout and meet my soon to be victim unknowingly to him. I called Khyail just to make sure he wasn't there.

"Hey baby." He said happy to hear from me.

"Hey love, what you up to?" I said.

"Nothing too exciting. I have a couple of meetings downtown to go to today. SO I should be downtown for the majority of the day. Let me know if you want to come grab lunch. We can go to your favorite restaurant Texas De Brazil if you like?"

"Aww I wish I could. I'm actually bogged down with appointments today. How about I just make you a special dinner tonight, besides you should be tired of Brazilian food." I said with a forced chuckle.

"That's even better baby. As long as you going to let me lick that pussy up for dessert." He said laughing.

"The good book does say to feed the hungry. I got you baby!" I said laughing.

After a few more laughs we said our goodbyes and went about our day.

I texted E to let him know that I was on the way. He texted back letting me know he was already there waiting. I pulled up to the gym workout clothes already on. As soon as I walked in the gym I noticed my soon to be victim, Brian on the stairmaster. After checking in at the front desk I sashayed my hips right on over to the stairmaster right next to him. He didn't have any headphones on which were a plus because that meant I could engage with him. I gave him a smile said hi and got on the machine. I noticed him taking a longer than normal gaze over my perky golden breasts sitting high in a black and lime green sports bra as his eyes slowly went down my body noticing my round perfectly shaped ass in my black workout leggings. He licked his lips.

"Hi how are you?" He said licking his lips again.

"I'm good. How do I work this machine? This is my first time here. I heard it was good for your butt." I said with a nervous giggle.

He hopped off his machine so quickly to come help me with mine. I acted helpless and he set me up right how it was supposed to go. He pretty much followed me throughout the gym as I went to each machine.

Women need to realize that you can literally get any man you want to show interest in you if you know what you're doing. It's all about confidence and playing into that man's ego. It might take a minute to figure out what drives his ego but after you do, they're like putty in your hands. You can manipulate them as you see fit. Well at least that's been my experience. We talked for a minute then I told him I had to leave. He insisted on giving me his number before I left.

I smiled as I typed it into my phone. I looked around. I had a feeling I was being watched. Nonetheless, I told him I had to go to work and I'll call him when I'm free. I walked out the door making sure he was paying attention to my ass as I sashayed seductively out the door. I couldn't wait to get my hands on him.

Not even three minutes later I was calling him.

"Hey gorgeous! You missed me so soon?!" He answered on the first ring.

"You're so funny. No, my car is acting stupid. You think you can come give me a boost real quick?" I said into the phone sounding worried.

"Oh of course baby! Lucky for you I have cables already in my car." He said excited to help.

"Of course you do. You seem like the type. But I already have cables. I'm a big girl." I said giggling. I already knew he had cables in the car. E already checked all that out for me.

"Yeah, a big girl who still needs my help?" He said with a smug grin.

"Yep! No shame in my game. But my car stopped just around back of the gym, a 2015 Black Escalade. Can you come now? I'm worried I'm going to be late for work." I said.

"Sure thing baby. I'm already walking out the door to find you."He said.

I hung up the phone and waited in the car for him to pull up. I ran my black leather gloved fingers over the steering wheel nervously waiting for everything to go down. I had this weird feeling like I was being watched. I looked at E through my passenger side window making sure he was in position and unseen. As always he was in position crouched down low near my passenger side rear tire so he wouldn't be seen when Ronald pulled up.

Ronald pulled up just about two feet away from the hood of my car. I watched him get out the car walking up to my window ever so smoothly. It's about to get real rough real soon. I thought with a sly grin.

"Hey Freckles. Where's the cables? I know you gotta get going…" He said as he approached the car.

"Oh they're still in the trunk. I didn't see the need on getting dirty baby." I said looking up with a giggle.

"Oh you're such a lady." He said teasing.

"Damn right!" I said with a laugh.

He proceeded to the trunk as I waited for the inevitable.

I heard a loud thump and I knew he had been knocked out. I listened as I heard another loud thud as E threw him in the back of the trunk. E hopped in the guy's car as he motioned for me to head on out. I drove off but I still had an eerie feeling like I was being watched. I turned out the gym and headed across the street to the Meijers. I let E go past me as he searched for a perfect spot to park his car. I parked up front in the handicap spot right in front of the door. I waited then watched as E walked into the store with his black baseball cap and all black sweatpants. I noticed he was still wearing his gloves and Tshirt. I waited another five minutes until he walked out in his white wife beater, black sweat pants. He no longer had the hat, black tee and gloves. He opened my car door and hopped in the seat.

"That went rather smoothly. Don't you think?" He said wiping his forehead with his red bandana.

I noticed the beads of sweat all over his body.

"I can't tell with all that sweating you doing." I said laughing.

"It wasn't that bad but we still have to get him locked up in my basement." I said with a hint of worry.

"Oh I got that. He's outta there. I let him breathe in that nice knock you out cocktail on the rag."

"Cool. I don't need any hiccups. I need everything to continue to go as smoothly as possible."

Just as quickly as I said that and was turning up my driveway I noticed Khyail's p2016 Dodge Charger parked right in my spot.

"Oh shit!" I exclaimed.

"Why the fuck is he here?" E took the words out my mouth.

"I don't know. But don't worry. I'll get rid of him." I said getting agitated.

I parked the car and hopped out to go to his car. He got out and immediately started walking towards my car.

"Who the fuck you got in there? Who are you? What the fuck is going on?" He yelled angrily.

"What's the problem?" I said thrown back and confused.

"You have someone in your trunk Lilly. What the hell is going on? I called the police." He said.

"YOU DID WHAT?" I yelled seeing red.

E opened the passenger door as soon as he heard police.

"Young dog you called the police? What type of guy are you? Lilly we gotta go. I told you to leave those cornballs alone."

"Ok…ok…calm down. I didn't call the police but I still want to know what's going on and if I don't like it then I will call them. I don't believe this shit." He said sounding extremely torn between right and wrong.

"You not gone call anybody, Young dog. This can go from you being curious to you being killed real quick. Now give me your phone so she can go talk to you." E shouted sounding real intimidating.

"I'm not…."Khyail began to say something but I cut him off.

"Come on Khyail give me your phone so we can go in the house and talk." I interrupted grabbing his phone.

I handed the phone to E.

"Make sure he didn't contact anyone. I'll handle this and you handle that." I said motioning to the man in the trunk.

"What do you mean handle it? Who the fuck are you Lilly?!" Khyail yelled.

"I'll explain everything when we get inside but I really need you to calm down. You're making me irritated and I'm already stressed out you know my body can't handle all that damn stress. You are throwing me off." I said as calmly as I could muster.

"Throwing you off?! Oh I'm sorry for throwing you off from kidnapping a grown ass man. Who does that?!" He yelled not backing down.

I pulled my gun out my jacket pocket gripping it close to my right side. He froze.

"You're so fucking stubborn! Just this once I need you to give me control or I'm going to fucking lose it. I will explain everything in a minute just let me figure out the words." I yelled.

His body stood frozen but I could tell he wanted to say "you mean the lies."

He followed me inside my purple front door down the corridor that leads to my living room. I took off my Northface hoodie, still keeping the gun in hand.

"You can put the gun down. I'm good. I ain't no killer baby. That's you." He said softly.

"Who said I was a killer?" I yelled getting angrier. What exactly did he know?

"I mean what are you doing this for Lilly? This is real life this isn't a Criminal Minds tv show. I swear to god we're you're not watching no more of them shows. Your crazy ass will apply it to your real life." He said almost in a whisper.

"What if I told you he was a child molester and he deserved it." I said in a whisper just like him.

"Who are you to determine that though?" He said getting slightly louder.

"The punishment of God." I said still whispering.

He laughed.

"You are a trip! It's a movie Lilly! A movie! It's not real!" He said in disbelief catching my reference to Blood and Bones with Michael Jai White.

I kicked off my black and gold addidas tennis shoes and raised my legs on the couch lying my feet onto his lap. I laid the gun beside me on the couch.

"Rub my feet please. I've had a crazy day... Nothing went as planned." I said laughing.

"This is serious Lilly. Stop fucking playing. What's going on?" He said concerned.

"I don't know Khyail. There is just some stuff you don't know about me. Shit, there's stuff I don't know about me." I said.

"Well you know why that man is in your trunk, don't you? And what does E have to do with all of this?" He said finally back to his normal tone of voice.

"He molested one of my patients. I wanted to make sure it never happened again." I said quietly.

"Ok but what about the police? What does it have to do with you?" He said sternly.

"I was molested before. I can't get my molesters but I can get theirs. I'm with it. It has a lot to do with me I guess." I said looking up into his eyes.

"Theirs? There is more than just him?" He said incredulously...

"Well yes, he's like the seventh. I have a whole list," I said laughing.

I was calming down. He no longer posed as a threat. He was rubbing my feet and genuinely just seemed to want to know what was going on. And who really was this woman he was so madly in love with. I didn't know what to tell him other than the truth.

"Lilly you can't be serious. Stop laughing and just be serious for a minute. The laughing makes you come off as a psychopath and I'm trying real hard not to believe that." He said still in amazement that his normally overly emotional girlfriend who cries over Disney movies was acting this cold and heartless when it came to someone else's life. I'm sure it seemed like all my humanity had been drained from me.

"Listen… I've killed seven men, five of which I did on my own. The other two, E did. They are all child molesters that got off on the system. I always give the system a chance to provide justice and when they don't I come through. I've never killed anyone who didn't deserve it and I stand by what I do."

"Okay, and what made you start?" He said curious.

"I don't know…. I never thought about it. I guess it was the journal that Mariee gave me. It was one of her patient's diary like book but the way the girl spoke through her words just resonated with me so much. It was like she was speaking through me. I just wanted to hurt those people. I wanted to kill them. I wanted to torture them. I felt compelled to kill." I said waiting for him to go on with his questions.

"And what does E have to do with it?" He said.

"E disposes the bodies and sells the body parts and helps if things get too crazy." I said actually rather relieved to be sharing my truth with him.

"Why would he do that for you?" He said as if he was jealous that another man would do something so risky for me.

"He owes me. It's his fault I'm this way." I whispered in a dazed glance.

"Snap out of it Lilly. I need to know what you know so I know how to help you!" He yelled shaking my feet.

"I would have never got molested. I would have never had my memory so completely destroyed from trying to repress so much fucked up shit that happened. I would not do such insane things searching for the truth. The truth about me! My truth! Why don't I know it?! I wouldn't be out here killing people for peace. My own peace that is." I rambled on.

"What would he have to do with all that?" Khyail asked.

"If he would have been a good father then none of the aforementioned would have ever happened. All he had to do was be a good father from the start. It's too little too late now." I said.

"Father….he's not even old enough to be your father. I thought you said he was your brother.

"I think you just assumed and I went with it. I never referred to him as anything other than E." I stated with certainty.

"Naw, you said you was introducing me to your bro E. You specifically said bro. I remember that shit." Khyail said with more certainty.

"Well maybe I did but I meant like that's my bro, homie, friend…not my actual brother." I said.

"What makes you think I would be cool with you hanging so closely with a bro, homie, friend or whatever the fuck? Why couldn't you have just said he was your father? I don't get it." He said sounding confused.

"He hasn't been a father. I don't feel right referring to him as that." I said.

"Well shit if you're not going to be honest with yourself at least be honest with me." He said.

"You don't know me Khyail so don't judge me. You're always so judgemental. Just chill on me. They deserved that shit and E owes me his help. Period." I said getting agitated.

"One day you'll realize no one owes you anything which is why people hardly ever get what they deserve. You gotta let that pain go. Forgive your father and work on you. Don't hold him to that guilt of his past mistakes. I'm certain he already holds himself to that guilt without your help. He is clearly trying his hardest to prove his love and loyalty to you. You can't grow like this baby. You can't." He said his eyes filling up with tears.

"Don't go there. You don't know. You've had a father hell both your parents all your life. You will never know. You have no idea how it feels to go without and everything that happened as a result of it. I know that's something I have to deal with when it comes to my father but we all have our demons. Let's not get started on yours."

Just then E walked in the room.

"He's secure in the basement. Is he good?" He said pointing at Khyail.

"I think so…. Wait let's see." I said as I looked over to him while an idea popped into my head.

I got up and grabbed his hand leading him downstairs into the basement. I almost fell as my feet glided across the floor in my black ankle socks. E followed behind us.

"I can't believe you're her father. Nice to remeet you I think."

"Yeah…Yeah….we'll see…" E said with a smirk on his face. He had figured out what I was up to.

Just then I gave him my gun as E pointed his gun at him.

"Shoot him." I said pointing to the guy securely chained in my basement. He was still in his grey sweatpant suit that was drenched from his nervous sweat from this day.

Bang! Bang!

He shot him twice with no hesitation.

I looked at him in shock.

"Ohmigod! How could you do that so easily without any serious thought?!" I said to him really surprised he did it.

"There's a lot you don't know about me too. Besides you said he was a child molester right?"

"Yeah…."

"So he deserved it." He said simply.

I had never been more in love then at that very moment. I ran up gave him a kiss and took the gun from him.

Thank you baby! You had me scared for a minute. I thought I was going to have to kill you." I said laughing.

"The really funny thing is that she's serious." E said with a chuckle.

Khyail looked at me straight in the eyes. I could feel my heart skip a beat.

"She was never serious. She knew I would always have her back whether she's right or wrong. Right?" He said still looking deeply into my eyes. "I was never going to call the police. I just wanted some answers." He said turning back towards E.

"Good cause I like you for her. It would have been a shame to have to get rid of you just cause you were being nosey." E said to Khyail.

I loved seeing them bond especially now that he knew E was my father. It just felt different. Maybe what he said made sense. I knew I needed to forgive my father but it was so much easier being mad at him. That was for another day though. I just wanted E to get rid of all this evidence and let me relax and enjoy my man for the night. He just killed for me.

"E, you got this right?" I said to E.

"You know it baby. Go relax. I know how you hate how plans suddenly up and change."

"Yes! Someone knows me! I'll be upstairs. Let yourself out…. Oh and thanks for being there." I said to E opening the door to go upstairs. Khyail followed behind me. I was ready for bed.

E looked up and you could see it all in his face that he needed to hear that.

"Anytime baby." He said watching us walk up the stairs.

I went straight up the second set of stairs to my bedroom and laid across my bed.

"You still have a lot more questions to answer but I'll let you answer them in the morning." Khyail said pulling my black work out pants down over my socks. He traced his finger along the lines of my panties, then quickly followed his finger with his tongue. I didn't care that my dad was right downstairs because at that moment all I wanted was my man inside me.

# Chapter Twelve

We were in the orphanage for another two weeks before there was a new family that wanted to try us out. This couple was very old, they were each in their fifties. The lady was really mean and the father was rather quiet. They had like five other kids in the house and there were only four bedrooms. They had one daughter of their own named Michelle who was off to college and only came home on some weekends. On paper I guess they didn't look so bad.

It seemed as if they made foster parenting out to be a real job with lots of benefits. Including the three of us they had 8 kids in the home. They only had 3 bedrooms and two bunk beds in each room. What irritated me about them in the beginning was that whenever the case worker or social worker would visit they would put these expensive comforter sets on the bed with these really nice bed skirts. They told them all these lies and prepped us on what to say to the case workers. It was ridiculous stuff about what we ate, where and how we played. It was absurd and all lies. The lady her name was Jewel, she was really mean and very heavy handed. If one of us did anything wrong then she would beat all of us with either her hand which they were really big heavy hands with excessively big fingers or her shoe. And when I say her shoe, I mean heeled shoes. She was really a bitter mean old woman. Her husband Roger wasn't any better. He was really nice when he was drunk but when he was sober and couldn't drink it was the worse. He always started cussing Jewel out about us kids and our toys being everywhere. I was really only close with her daughter who would often help me write letters to my own dad in prison whenever she came home from college. I was in that house for quite some time. It was the longest time spent in a foster home so far. It had been almost 2 years now and I was getting used to never seeing my real mother and father again. I accepted the truth that I was alone and it was just my brothers and I. We managed to have two different caseworkers who both remained oblivious to the abuse that was going on in that home. One of the two, Michael Overton seemed to think something was up but he was unable to prove anything I guess because we remained in the house. I experienced so many different things in that house. I got my first flu, chicken pox, learned how to tie my shoes, and found out that I was legally blind and needed glasses. I was in that house for a little over a year. The whole time I was there Roger, Jewel's husband who was drunk far often than not would be waiting in the shower at any given night that she had me go in to shower. I didn't scream. I didn't say no. I just stood there in silence and let him do what he wanted to do to me.

157

I assumed that the foster dads were allowed to do this. This was what was supposed to happen. If not, then why was no one there to protect me and say it was wrong? My brother Michael caught him sneaking out my shower and asked me about it. I told him it was nothing. I guess he knew better because later that night he took a knife and cut right underneath his eye. However, when Jewel seen it she just cleaned it up and put a band aid on it. The next night Michael took perm out the fridge and spread it all over his eye. He had to get rushed to the hospital which immediately opened a child protective case. After a couple of months of Michael being gone they came and got Antonio and I as well. I don't know if that was his intent but he would always get us out of a crazy home.

I woke up all the way on the other side of the bed far away from Khyail. I could never cuddle longer than an hour. I would always get uncomfortable and want my space. Thankfully, my bed was big enough to do that. I looked over at Khyail with his mouth all open , snoring all loud and completely passed out sleep. You wouldn't believe we had just kidnapped and killed a man the day before. He seemed to have had a peaceful sleep. I know I was a mess after my first kill. I couldn't sleep for days. It made me wonder just how much about him I didn't know.

I began to read the diary after waking up. I quickly put it down after reading those pages because I just couldn't take anymore. It felt all too familiar and I would always get gooscbumps and this tingly feeling while my heart felt like it was going to beat out my chest. I always had to calm myself down after reading it. I had to figure some things out. I knew I had to do something about Stephanie but what? Her mother seemed just as bad as the step dad. I wanted to kill them both. I was still a little irritated about Khyail popping up when he did because I really wanted to try torturing out. I laughed to myself. How am I over here mad because I didn't get a chance to torture someone?

Sounds crazy. And being a psychologist myself I would definitely know crazy. But it was my truth; I wanted a chance to torture a child molester. Death seemed far too kind of a punishment. I also needed to take the time out and have a talk with Mariee over this diary. I needed more info. Every time I read about another one of her devils, I wanted to kill them too. Of course I couldn't tell Mariee that but I was definitely going to get some information up out of her. She told me not to consult with her about the journal until I was finished with the entire book but I couldn't take it anymore. I needed all the information she had. I just didn't know how I was going to get it.

# *Chapter Thirteen*

Weeks went by and still no mention of the last guy I killed on the news. I knew he was a loner but still it seemed odd. I seen Andrew on there once but the buzz soon died down. I had a talk with E, my father, and finally forgave him. We had actually grown to a better place. I thank Khyail for that.

I was meeting regularly with Stephanie and I was beginning to grow especially fond of her. She reminded me so much of me. I couldn't wait to see her later today but I was feeling guilty for allowing her to continue to be where she was at. I filed paperwork with Child Protective Services to report my findings and recommendations but that was two weeks ago and still nothing had been done to remove her from her parents. I was becoming fed up and was really ready to take matters into my own hands. Khyail told me he didn't want me doing that anymore because it simply wasn't safe for me. He spoke of other ways I can help the children without directly putting myself in danger. I felt invincible and knew that I had it under control but I promised him I would stop and go back to counseling. But I didn't know if I would be able to keep that promise.

I walked into the lobby of my practice and Stephanie was already sitting in the chair with her nanny. Stephanie's mom had stopped bringing her about two weeks ago. Shortly after she found out about my psych report. She wanted nothing other than to take Stephanie to a new psychologist but it was court ordered for Stephanie to finish her counseling with me. However, the courts weren't doing anything about putting them in jail. They said it wasn't enough evidence. I was so tired of hearing that excuse.

"Hey Stephanie! How you doing?" I said grabbing Stephanie's hand and leading her back to our therapy room. She let go of my hand and gave me a big hug.

"I'm fine. Ms. Lilly! I missed you! She said squeezing me extra tight.

"I missed you too Stephanie." I said picking her up and sitting her down on the couch.

"I wish I could live with you Ms. Lilly." Stephanie said softly throwing me for surprise.

"I didn't know you felt that way Stephanie! I wish you could too. I would love that but I don't think it's possible." I said wondering if it was really possible.

Suddenly, Stephanie burst into tears.

"But I can't take it anymore. I can't. I want to just die sometimes.

All of a sudden a flashback popped into my head. It was me as a little girl hair in two long messily braided pigtails with a bloody nightgown on. I was curled in a ball on the bed feeling like I wanted to die. My heart started beating super fast feeling like it was going to pop out of my chest. I started grabbing my body as I felt the physical pain of that moment just as I felt the emotional pain. Beads of sweat started forming on my breasts peeking through my peach camisole underneath my cream blouse.

"Ms. Lilly! Ms. Lilly! Are you okay?!" I heard Stephanie say through my daze. I looked down she was pulling on my leg scared that something was wrong with me. I snapped out of it and grabbed her tight.

"I know how you feel baby. I'm going to make it happen. Some way I will. Don't worry. What about your mom? You would be okay with leaving her?" I asked curious to hear her response.

"Yes!!! She doesn't love me Ms. Lilly. She only loves herself. I don't want to deal with them anymore. She only got worse now that I've been spending time with you."

"What do you mean worse?" I asked feeling myself getting angry.

"She hits on me more and now she tells me to go in the room with him whenever I'm getting on her nerves. She knows what he does and just doesn't care. How can she not care for her own daughter?" Lilly said with tears rolling down her cheeks.

It reminded me of something the girl said in the diary I was reading. I knew something had to be done fast and I think I was just going to have to do it. I didn't have time to think of a full and complete plan.

"Stephanie ask your mom if you can stay over your friends tonight. I'm going to try and get this handled tonight. Are you sure you want to live with me? It would be forever." I said to Stephanie caressing her face as I wiped her tears away.

"I do want to live with you forever. I want you to be my mom now so I can be safe. Can you make that happen?" She said looking up into my eyes.

"I'm sure I can." I said confidently as an idea popped into my head.

"Listen Stephanie, I'm going to try and do it tonight so if you can go over your friend's house then definitely try but if not I'll make provisions for you to stay with my aunt for a couple hours while I handle things with your parents." I told her wrapping up my paperwork to end our session.

"Are they going to be okay?" She asked me timidly.

"I don't know. You want them to be?" I asked her curious to know.

"I want him to hurt like I hurt and I want her to know what it feels like for the one person that's supposed to save her to not care." She said solemnly.

My heart longed for her. How many more were living just like her? Traumatized and heart frozen from the pain.

"Then I'll do just that." I said giving her the assurance she needed in that moment even though I myself wasn't confident I could pull it off..

I walked her out the office and handed her off to her nanny.

"See you later on Stephanie. Be ready."

I watched them walk out the door then hurried up and grabbed my coat so I can leave.

"Wait…. Lilly are you about to leave? I wanted to talk to you. We haven't had a real talk in awhile now. How you doing? You been good?" Mariee asked running out her office after me.

"Yeah, just been really busy. I do need to talk to you though. About that girl's diary…..But not now I got something I gotta do tonight. But soon….You're a trip." I said with a forced chuckle walking out the door.

I'm a trip? What you mean? You must have figured it out?" Mariee said with a look of excitement on her face.

"Figured what out? I was talking about how deep the book was. It's bringing out a side of me that I don't know." I said wondering what she meant.

"Oh.....ok... Well wait what do you mean a different side of you?" Mariee said concerned.

"I can't talk about it right now Mariee....but tomorrow we'll catch up for brunch around eleven at our usual spot....Sound good?" I asked her eager to cut this conversation short.

"Alright! Alright!....see your fast ass later. Probably going to go do something nasty with Khyail right now. Busy my ass!" Mariee said with humorous disdain.

I laughed as I slammed the door to my office building shut behind me. I loved Mariee but I had to go. I had things to do. I had to call E and see if we could pull this off tonight.

"Hey, You free to go tonight" I asked as soon as I heard him pick up and say hello.

"Her parents?" He asked eagerly.

"Yeah. 10pm. I'll send further info to your email." I said before hanging up.

Truthfully, I couldn't stand knowing Stephanie was in the predicament as long as she was. I just didn't know what to do that would keep Stephanie from having to end up in foster care like I was. But I think I now have a plan that would keep both promises I made to Stephanie.

---

E and I pulled up to Stephanie's house and parked across the street exactly two houses away. I was fully dressed in all black and so was he. I turned over the rock in the back rose garden and sure enough the key was right inside it just as Stephanie said. Quietly I unlocked the back door and E and I slipped right on through as quiet as can be. It was completely dark in the house except for the upstairs bedroom. Clearly they were in there. I creeped up the stairs as E trailed behind me. I noticed the door cracked to the master room but I only saw Stephanie's mom in there laying in bed watching Criminal Minds. The irony I thought. He must not be home yet. I didn't even think of that. That's why you gotta plan.

"Stay here I'm going to go get Stephanie and get her somewhere safe." I whispered to E motioning for him to stay right on the other side of her door to keep watch out for her mother.

I made my way to what must be her room it was the only room with the bedroom shut. Every other room I could clearly see was unoccupied. I stopped in my tracks as I got closer to the door. I heard the faintest noise. Almost like a cat whimpering. I knew exactly what it was!

I kicked open the door gun in hand. As soon as I saw him I instantly became enraged. There he was on top of her as if she was his wife. I was seeing red.

"What the fuck?!" He yelled jumping off the bed from inside her. "Who the fuck are you?" He yelled trying to pull his boxers up.

"Your worst nightmare." I said seething with anger.

"Bitch please." He said laughing eerily coming towards me..

"Please what? Please kill me. Please rape me. Please burn me to ashes." E said coming through the door with Stephanie's mother with the gun pointed at her head. Get your ass on in there girl you sent your daughter with him. Wouldn't you like to see what he's been doing to her?" E went on pushing her mother inside the room as he yelled.

Ms. Lilly!!! I can't believe you came. Stephanie said with excitement as tears were still rolling down her cheeks.

"You knew I would baby." I said walking towards her to cover her up.

"I got her. Get him." I told E. I took off my backpack and pulled out my handcuffs. I cuffed her to bed post of Stephanie's daybed.

"You really are going to do this in front of my daughter?" She asked scared out her mind.

"You just might be the most ironically idiotic person I know. Your man is in front of your daughter doing all types of things to her while you lay in the other room watching criminal minds of all the shows to watch." I said thinking about what Khyail said.

"And now you have the audacity to be worried about what's happening in front of your daughter. Are you serious? Do you see the irony or is it just me?" I said still seething in anger.

"Don't judge me bitch." She said looking at me with a mix of fear and anger in her eyes.

"That's exactly what I'm going to do. This may be the one time that phrase is truthful. Because not only am I

172

judging you but I'm also going to sentence you to the punishment for your crime. You might as well address me as your honor." I said ready to knock her head off.

"You're insane. I knew I never should have bought her to you." She said.

"That might be the best thing you've ever done for her." I said watching as E finished securing him to the other side of Stephanie's bed.

"Come on Stephanie. You're coming with me baby. Get anything you really, really want. I'll buy you everything else. I need to get you out of here baby." I said picking her up out the bed.

"I already packed my bag Ms Lilly." She said pointing under the rocking chair in her room.

"You already did what? How could you leave me here?" Stephanie's mother said looking at Stephanie with tears in her eyes.

"How could you?" Stephanie said grabbing my hand as we walked out the door not at all looking back at her mother.

"From the mouth of babes....isn't that what they say? I'll be back E. I know you got this." I said looking at Stephanie's mom.

"See you soon hun!" I said to her with a wink.

I hurried up and left their house with Stephanie in my arms so I could take her to my aunt's house where I knew she would be safe.

I couldn't wait to come back though.

Brrrr! Brrr! Brrr! My phone vibrated in my pocket. I took it out and saw that it was Khyail.

"Yes baby?" I said nervously.

"Where you at? Why you not at home?" Khyail asked suspiciously.

"Why are you being a stalker?" I asked forcing out a laugh.

I had just pulled back up to Stephanie's house and I really needed to figure out how to get out of this conversation.

I just wanted to surprise you. That's all. Sorry for trying." He said sounding defeated.

"I don't like those kind of surprises. I like surprise gifts not surprise pop ups baby. I'm out with Mariee for the night. I won't be back till well after three." I said hoping he would get the hint.

"Oh that's fine baby. I'll just wait here for you. I know where the key is." He said eagerly.

"I prefer you not. I'm kind of having a ladies night. She more than likely we'll be too drunk to drive home so she'll stay the night with me. Is that cool?" I said hoping that lie would be sufficient.

"I guess baby. I kinda just wanted to see you. We doing breakfast or something tomorrow for sure." He said sounding disappointed.

175

"Ok baby. Talk to you tomorrow." I said thankful he bought it. I hung up the phone and walked up the driveway unlocking the door to Stephanie's old house.

The house was still as dark as it was when I left with Stephanie. I walked up the stairs to the only lit room in the house. There they were still handcuffed to the bed, Stephanie's mom on one end with her step dad on the other. E was sitting in the rocking chair watching ESPN on the 36 inch tv that sat on Stephanie's white dresser.

"Finally. I was getting tired of hearing them bitch back and forth. You ready to get started baby?" E said looking up at me from the tv.

"You already know!" I said with a smirk.

"So firstly, Stephanie is going to live with me because I can offer her a stable and safe home and you all clearly are unable to." I said addressing Stephanie's mom and step dad, The Reeds.

"Secondly, you have a choice on whether you want to live or die it is completely up to you but know that regardless of what your choice is I am going to get what I want. So it would behoove you to be smart.

Thirdly, and this one may be the hardest for you two, but you will both feel exactly what Stephanie felt and I mean that. Now do I have any questions?" I asked serenely.

"You are a psychotic bitch!" Stephanie's mom yelled.

"I might be. At least I'm nothing like you. What about you, Mr. Reed? Do you have any questions?"

"Just kill me and get it over with." He mumbled without looking up from the floor.

"Oh that would be too easy. I have great plans for you sir." I said going up to him and pushing his head down playfully. "Now which one of you wants to go first." I said with a demonic smile.

"Go first? What are you going to do to us?" Stephanie's mom questioned.

"Oh....... Just the same thing you let him do to your daughter. Now get up!" I yelled pulling her up from the floor after I watched the fear flood her eyes.

"E hand me the bag. Inside I had my black leather glamaholic duffle bag filled with everything we needed for the day. I unzipped it and pulled out another medium sized bag big enough to hold a pair of shoes.

E uncuffed Mr. Reed and used another pair of handcuffs as he cuffed each one of his hands to each bed post. He then pulled another two pair of hand cuffs cuffing each foot to the bottom legs of the bed. Surprisingly, Mr. Reed wasn't saying anything. It was almost as if he had given up and accepted his fate, whatever he thought it was.

"Now you will pick something out of this little bag and come over here with your sick little man." I said taking the cuffs off of Stephanie's mom and pushing the bag into her arms. E already had the gun aimed at her. I watched her look into the bag then look up at me with a shock."

178

"Yes honey. Dildos. Are you that much of a prude that you don't know what they are? Is that why your man won't stay in your room instead of going to go hurt her daughter." I said with disdain.

"What do you want me to do with it?" She said looking at it as if it was the scariest thing she's ever seen.

"Oh. Great question. I'm glad you asked. I would hate for you to be confused. You're going to rape him." I said to her matter of factly.

"Do what?!" Both of them yelled in unison.

"I want you to rape him. To be clear I want you to sodomize him! Until he bleeds." I said sternly.

Just then Mr. Reed started bucking like crazy trying to get free from his handcuffs.

"Be still boy." E said knocking him upside the head with his gun. He groaned as he struggled from keeping himself from folding over the bed.

"Now you get behind him and shove that dildo up his ass." I yelled getting pissed everything was taking so long.

Slowly she walked over to him.

"Do it!" I yelled.

She inched down his pants. I pushed his body over as far as it could bend with the handcuffs.

"Ram it up there." I yelled.

I hand cuffed her left hand to the bed while keeping her right hand out.

"E you can go. I got this for the moment." I said to E knowing he didn't want to see this.

E left the room. I reached in the bed and pulled out a leather whip. I whipped it real hard across her shoulders. It also hit the side of her cheek. She screamed out in pain.

"I said do it!" I yelled louder.

She rammed it inside him so hard.

"Keep going!" I yelled as I kept cracking my whip against both their skin. Oddly, he was silent with not much to say just a painful grimace every time it went inside him or I cracked the whip against his skin. She kept a steady pace for fear that she would get hit by the hip. I kept cracking the whip letting out all of my frustration. They were both bleeding out the slashes the whip left on their skin. I didn't want to stop. I kept going and going as flashback after flashback popped into my head. I started to get dizzy as I felt my heart beating as if it was going to explode out my chest. Stephanie's room seemed to transform into a room I remembered growing up in as a child. Just then I seen a figure coming towards me. He was Indian with a long silky black ponytail and a motorcycle jacket. I felt myself shaking as the man kept coming towards me.

Lilly! Lilly! Snap out of it!" I opened my eyes as E was shaking me.

Mr. Reed's pants were back up and he was folded over the bed bleeding everywhere. Stephanie's mom was sitting on the floor back handcuffed to the bed.

"My bad. I lost it for a second." I said trying to get my eyes to focus and stop being so blurry.

"No problem. You just had me scared for a minute. You were beating them to a pulp and screaming out stop. What was that about?" He said.

"I'll be back. I need to get myself together." I said running out the room leaving out to go to the bathroom.

"Yeah. I'll be back too. Get ready girl, it's your turn next. I finally get to have some fun." E said to Stephanie's mom with a wink.

He left the room to follow me to the bathroom.

"What happened in there?" He asked me worried.

"I don't know man. I completely lost it. Like I started having flashbacks then I just blacked out."

"Well we don't have that much more left. Can you handle it? I knew we shouldn't have been doing all of this." He asked genuinely concerned.

"I got it. If I want Stephanie this is what I have to do." I said confidently as I splashed the last bit of water on my face.

"Now get up!" E walked into the room yelling at Stephanie's mom adjusting his belt to his pants.

She stumbled to her feet as quickly as she could. I could tell she was in a lot of pain.

"Are you going to rape me?" She asked as her voice trembled.

"Exactly, what I'm going to do." He said as he pushed her up against the bed beside her husband who was still bent over the bed.

"Now take off your pants." He said quietly. I could see how uncomfortable he was.

She slowly inched her pants down with her free hand.

"Your panties too." He ordered.

She stood there butt ass naked, her body shaking in fear as I watched the goose bumps pop up on her sun tanned skin.

E got closer to her to where he was right behind her. He pulled her into his groin as he grabbed her neck.

"I could never rape anybody. I'm not a sick pathetic piece of trash like the man you married and chose over your own daughter. You deserve to be raped to know how she felt and what she'll now have to deal with for the rest of her life. But your karma will come for you. I've done some foul shit but I can't even have this on my conscious. I don't see how you can." He whispered in her ear then walked away as he fastened the belt buckle back to his pants."

I watched her let out a sigh of relief. I wish she could get raped. The fear she felt in that moment was nothing compared to the fear Stephanie had embedded in her for the past three years.

"So now that I've got your attention, this is what we're going to do." I said loudly jerking everyone's attention towards me. "You're going to confess to raping your stepdaughter on this video camera." I said motioning his head towards the direction of the video camera.

"And you mam…You're going to confess to knowing about it and often sending your husband in the room to rape your daughter." I said looking into her eyes glaring in disgust.

"Then you will let us go?" She asked with hope in her eyes."

"That's to be determined. Only if you sign your parental rights over to me, relocate to another state, and never speak of this to anyone or try to contact her ever again."

"Ok we'll do whatever you want, as long as you'll let us go." She said assuredly sounding more hopeful now that she knew there was a possibility of her making it out alive.

"Sure thing." I said ready to get this over it and get in my bed..

I pulled the "Release of Child" court document out of the bag for her and her husband to sign. I handed it to her directing her where to place their signatures. I had already filled out my information so that the child would be released to me for adoption.

"Now you have 21 days" to request a hearing. Do I need to keep you somewhere safe for 21 days or can I expect full compliance to this matter.

"We're not going to say anything. Honestly, I'm glad she's gone. I get to spend more time with my husband." She said looking over at her husband still slumped over the bed.

He didn't make a sound.

"You're pathetic." I told her rolling my eyes.

"Another thing, you have to leave the state once everything is finalized. We don't ever want to see you again. Am I clear?" I added.

"Crystal clear. Just take her and leave us alone." She said looking down at her hands.

"Good. And if there are any issues this video will become viral. But of course that will be the least of your worries." I said taking the paperwork from her hand and putting it back into my bag.

I threw her keys to the handcuffs and walked out the door. E was already at the bottom of the stairs waiting for me. We walked out the door. I was so thankful the plan went smoothly without a hitch. That's how I knew God was on my side. I always made it out without so much as a scratch. If what I was doing was so bad then why was God always there watching over me to make sure I was safe?

I got in the car and dialed my aunt.

"Hey girl. Did you have fun?" My aunt answered on the second ring.

"Huh? Whatchu mean?" I said caught off guard by her answering so quick.

"Salsa dancing silly. Did you have fun?" She asked again.

I had completely forgot that I told her we had already bought tickets for the salsa dancing class when my friend asked me to watch my god daughter, Stephanie. Luckily, my aunt didn't mind watching Stephanie for me while I handled her parents.

"Yeah yeah! We had a good time. I got some moves for you when you're ready." I said with a little laugh cleaning up the fact that I forgot my lie.

"How is she?" I asked her after common pleasantries were exchanged.

"She's fine. Sleep. You coming to get her now? You know you can wait." She said assuredly.

"Oh no. She'll freak out if she doesn't wake up to me. I'm on my way right now. Have her ready if you can. See you soon." I said.

"Ok baby. I will. See you when you get here." She said hanging up the phone.

"You okay baby?" My dad asked nudging me on the cheek after noticing the peaceful look in my eyes.

"I think so. I find it amazing how everything is working for my good. It's like I have a guardian angel coming through for me every time. But the way I feel? That's what doesn't make sense. I'm enjoying this. Thoroughly. What would only make this feel any better was if I was hurting the people who actually hurt me as a child. That would make me feel like I was all powerful and vindicated to say the least. It would take away the lack of power I felt from when they hurt me to well….pretty much all my life. I mean to know you were molested by four different men and have no idea who they are or any total recollection of the memory. To randomly have flashbacks is beyond scary. Just last week Khyail bought some orange Dial soap home and the first night I took a shower with it I had the wildest flashback of that old man in the shower. In my dreams the people never have any faces, it was the same way in the flashbacks. Just eyes. But those eyes glaring down at me when I turned around in the shower. His naked body. His arms suddenly wrapped tight around my waist. That? That felt so real. My body would start shaking, felt like my heart was going to beat out my chest, and I would get goose bumps all over my body. It would only last for a moment, a brief second. Just long enough to give me that overwhelming sense of fear. And the flashback was brought on by something as simple as soap. I still use that soap with hopes I'll get more flashbacks. I just want to know the full story not bits and pieces of my life. I just wish I could remember it all."

"I feel you baby girl. I wish I could have done something to help you. I was so young and ignorant. My heart was in the right place but my mind couldn't keep up." My daddy said looking over into my eyes.

"I know daddy. Don't worry. We're good now." I said with certainty.

We picked up Stephanie and drove to my house. She was already dressed and still sleep when we got there. When we got to my house I carried her up to my guest room and tucked her in. My dad brought the bag inside, gave me a hug and headed out to his motorcycle to go home. I was thankful for him on this day more than ever. Stephanie was going to give me my life back, hopefully my sanity too. She gave me a reason to live. I was blessed to be a blessing to her. In a sense saving her has saved me.

I stripped down to my purple lace bra and panty set leaving my black jeans, tee, and boots in the middle of the floor. My all black Glock Nine resting on the table beside

191

my wine glass. I filled the cup all the way up with barely an inch to spare. I walked up to my room peering into Stephanies's room as I passed it. She was sleep still tucked in as tight as I had her. This may be her most peaceful night's sleep in quite some time now I thought as I kept walking into my room hopping into my bed after grabbing the book off my nightstand.

# *Chapter Fourteen*

*That was a lot Lilly. Now what about your relationships*

*with men?*

*My relationships with men have always been strange.*

*Well, I should say boys because they hadn't quite matured*

*into men yet as I hadn't even grown into a woman. I'm 25*

*years old now and I think that out of all the guys I've dated,*

*I only had three guys that I would consider grown men.*

*One I'm with now, One I threw away for the pettiest of*

*reasons, and the other I simply destroyed emotionally.*

*However, In my defense, he started it. I used to have such a*

*strong desire to get revenge on anyone whoever hurt me. I
still do.*

**What do you mean?**

*My relationships with guys just began when I was
seventeen. Up until then I had always been extremely
curious about guys but scared as hell because of what I
went through in my childhood. I did have a relationship
back in the seventh grade but it was nothing major just that
puppy love stuff they always talk about in movies. That boy
begged me to be with him every single day of school for
three months until I finally said yes. And boy when I tell
you that the moment I said yes he was like a lost puppy
attached to my hip. I really didn't understand it. I mean
now I'm gorgeous now but back then I looked a mess. I
mean I was bony as hell, I had freckles, braces, a crazy
pigeon toed/bow-legged walk. I looked ridiculous to myself,
I could only imagine how I looked to everyone else. But I
guess beauty is truly in the eyes of the beholder. The boy's*

*name is Chris but everybody called him Zane. He was in the eighth grade. However, we went to a private Lutheran school so the seventh and eighth grade class was a conjoined class. He was the most popular boy in the school. He was an amazing athlete and he actually had a nice little body to be an eighth grader. When it came to physical connection all we ever did was hug. I was scared of doing anything else but he didn't know that. When I first met him I told him that I already had sex with three boys and he just didn't seem worth my time. I would have been recklessly teased if I would have said I was a virgin so I lied. No girl at that school was a virgin, unless we were all lying which now that I think back on it, I think we all were lying. I remember we used to get dressed for gym and we used to take turns kissing each other to try and get better at our kissing. That's what we told each other. But I think we really didn't know what we were doing because we hadn't actually ever kissed a guy before. It got a little ridiculous.*

*Every girl in our class was kissing each other. We definitely like doing it because it escalated from the gym locker room, to the hallways, to even in class just kissing. I'm surprised we didn't get mono. Zane used to get so mad because I hadn't even kissed him yet, not even a peck and here I was kissing girls right in front of his face. I was scared of anything the slightest bit intimate with him. Boys scared me. I just felt more comfortable kissing a girl. She was just as weak as me and most of all she couldn't shove anything inside of me. Not to mention, it was nothing more than a kiss. There were no emotions and no one trying to control me. I ended up stopping with the whole kissing girls thing because people were making fun of Zane and only I could do that. And I started feeling a tingling sensation when I was kissing them. I guess we had finally got it right. However, I wasn't trying to turn in to no lesbian so that shit had to stop. I didn't have any real feelings for Zane. I loved the attention and I didn't even have to do anything to get it. He, on the other hand, seemed to be head over heels for me. Christmas time came up and our class did the whole secret santa thing. Zane went as far as to trade with someone else so he can have me. Of course, I didn't know at the time hence the secret santa part. But for that whole week I was only getting warheads and reese cups which were my favorite candies at the time. Now, I was happy about the candy but everyone else was getting notebooks and cute little pens. I was getting pissed that I was only getting candy and of course I complained to Zane about it and he was making fun of me and flaunting his cheap little gifts so I was getting even more pissed. When it came time to reveal that he was my secret santa he revealed himself and I was seriously contemplating breaking up with him. But everyone else seemed to know something that I didn't. They were all like you're going to be all over Zane when you see what he has in store for you. They were like you might even kiss him and started laughing. Well later on that* day we had our Christmas production. Everybody and their family were going to be there. I was curious to see what he was going to do.

Only my adopted mom came so that was good because it would have been some serious social suicide if my adopted father was there. Well, the production was going really well. Then Zane did his Christmas rap and it was supposed to be over. But after his rap he called me to the middle of the stage. His mother then brought me a tiara and gave me two boxes and then went back to her seat. Zane opened the boxes then told me to close my eyes. He then proceeded to put a watch on my wrist and a necklace around my neck. After that he told me to open my eyes. He then did this little rap about me and ended it with "Merry Christmas Beautiful." I was thoroughly overwhelmed, embarrassed, and pleased. I gave him the usual hug, said thank you, then I went back to my place in the production. I couldn't believe he planned all this for me and had all these people in on it. All of my classmates said I wasn't shit basically because I didn't kiss him. They said I should be grateful for who I have and what I got and that they would do anything for a guy like him. I didn't talk to Zane till that next Monday as it was the weekend. He was hurt too. He was acting so distant and we sat right next to each other. I asked him what the problem was and he said that I was a cold person and I had no heart. I said "why, because you didn't get your kiss? He said no then went on with all this bullshit about me not showing any type of affection towards him, we don't talk on the phone and I don't really want to be with him. He even went on to say that he was a fool for making me his girl. I didn't want to lose my social status in school so I told him I loved him and I kissed him on the lips. It was like a one second kiss and I don't even count it as my first kiss but it meant the world to him. It's funny how people can share a moment, the same exact moment and have completely different feelings towards that moment.

*Well after I said that he felt like we were going to get married or something. He was ridiculously sweet and good to me. But all good things soon come to an end.*

*There was this guy that came to the school in the middle of the year. His name was Andrew. He had been kicked out of all public schools and now he was here with us. Andrew was obnoxious, conceited, and perverted. Zane didn't like him at all. I think he felt threatened because Andrew was also really good at basketball too. Well one day I was in the hallway on my way to the office and he came up behind me. He pulled me to him with his hands on my hips. He then moved his hands so that they were literally palming my ass cheeks. I had on the normal catholic girl uniforms so I had on this pleated skirt with a white button up top. It actually felt good but who was he to have his hands on my ass? I told him to get his hands off on me and pulled away. He let me go but said "You liked it. Zane can't make you feel the way I do and you know that." I went to the office* and went back to class as if nothing happened. However, I was thinking that Zane never did touch me like that. He never even tried. All hewanted was a kiss. In my warped mind it made me think that Andrew desired me more than Zane did. I was confused.

About a week later I got another hall pass to go to the restroom. I''m guessing Andrew got a hallpass as well because seconds after I walked into the bathroom Andrew did as well. He pushed me into a stall up against the wall. He started kissing the back of my neck with his hands squeezing my already C cup breasts. He started biting the sides of my neck. I was actually moaning! He had his finger inside my panties as he was massaging my clit. His penis was so hard rubbing against my booty cheeks. I was scared but turned on all at the same time. It brought back memories, so many memories. Tears started falling down my cheeks. He told me to stop crying and stop fighting because I liked it. He said if I didn't like it then his *finger wouldn't be so wet. He pulled his finger out and shoved it in my mouth. I was dripping wet and I couldn't understand it. Why was I so wet? Why was my body tingling like this yet I was so scared? It all stopped when a girl walked into the bathroom. She went in her stall and he walked out of mine and out of the bathroom all together. I sat on the toilet seat for about ten more minutes then got up rinsed my face off, made sure I looked decent and went back to class again like nothing ever happened. I walked in he held his finger to his lips to warn me to be quiet then flashed his evil grin. I felt like I had a sign on my head that said "I'm weak and I want you to rape me."*

*By the age of twelve I had been molested by now four different people. There had to be something wrong with me. I went home that night and gyrated on my pillow until I came. I was masturbating to the thought of Andrew taking me. At some point can rape turn into consensual sex? I was scaring myself with how much I masturbated. It felt like I needed to or my pussy would literally pulsate as if it had*

*it's own separate heartbeat. I was always wet but I was*

*scared of boys, petrified really.*

*Zane and I ended up breaking up after my adoptive father*

*ended up threatening his life for no reason other than he*

*was speaking to me in front of him. That was the first flag*

*from my adoptive father but there were many more to*

*come. The next day Zane had moved his desk away from*

*mine. He was hurt because I didn't tell my adopted father*

*about us. He didn't understand that that wasn't really an*

*option. So my very first relationship ended and I was stuck*

*being a nobody again, a bony little girl with freckles and*

*braces. From my ended relationship came ended*

*friendships because we shared friends of course. Since he*

*was the popular one, I became the hated one. Good thing*

*there was only one more month left of school. I kind of*

*wished Andrew was still at the school. At least he would*

*have acted like he liked me. Pitiful huh? Andrew had left*

the school two weeks after our "little thing." He had actually been kicked out for assaulting the principle. It was just me and I became a serious bookworm that last month, extra credit and all that. My seventh grade report card was real nice! Over the summer I watched the news faithfully because I just loved staying up to date on current events. However, this particular day, I couldn't believe what I saw. A mugshot of Andrew was shown on the screen for him being arrested for raping a thirteen year old little girl. I found out that Andrew was actually sixteen. He must have been held back quite a few years. They showed a video of the police walking with him in handcuffs and Andrew had that same evil grin resting on his face that scared the shit out of me. My adoptive mom asked me what was wrong and I simply said nothing, he just went to school with me. I went to the bathroom and vomited up the entire contents of my stomach. I felt so horrible. I could have been the one to prevent that little girl from being hurt. If only I would have *told my story. This was all my fault. I just kept hearing him*

*say whatever, you liked it" over and over in my head. I*

*wonder if she had got that same tingly sensation that I got*

*when he touched me? Or was I just this sick and twisted*

*little girl? I wonder if he ever stopped touching on girls*

*who didn't want to be touched by him? He seemed to like*

*turning someone on who didn't want him. It couldn't just*

*be SEX because he had an abundance of girls who wanted*

*him and threw themselves at him yet he chose the ones who*

*didn't want him. He wanted the power of taking what he*

*was being denied. I don't understand guys like him at all.*

*Well, after my seventh grade year I stayed away from the*

*idea of guys and relating to them past the point of a*

*friendship level. I honestly didn't even trust being friends*

*with them because I felt all boys had ulterior motives. I*

*questioned the way I looked at them and how I interacted*

*with them. I felt like I had to of been doing something to*

*lead them on and make it seem like it was okay to take*

205

*advantage of me. But with all that I was still sick and twisted in my own right. Not to the detriment of others but I was just super sexual all the time. I masturbated daily and would fantasize about having sex and how it would feel with someone who actually loved me as opposed to doing it with someone who was only trying to hurt me.*

I stopped reading. I put the book down and walked out the room into my home gym. I put on my gloves and punched that bag as tears ran down my cheeks. I was crying harder than I ever have before. My tears ran down my cheeks dripping down my breasts. I was upset. I was angry.

I picked up my phone and dialed Mariee.

"What the hell is this?" I yelled into the phone through my tears.

"What do you mean? What's going on? Why are you crying?" She asked sounding concerned but half sleep.

"This book you gave me. It's me isn't it?" I yelled a little longer.

"Wait. What?" She asked sounding confused.

"ANSWER ME!!! Who is this book about? Is this me?

Am I telling the story? Stop fucking playing with me Mariee. Who is it?" I said a little quieter remembering I now had a child in the other room sleeping.

"It's 1:32 in the am Lilly. Can't this wait till the morning?" Mariee said groggily.

"No, it can't. I just finished the most tragic rawest book I've ever read in my life and once I finished that book that you gave me to read I realized it was me that was telling the story all along. How could I not know it was me? How could you not tell me?" I said angrily into the phone.

"You were hypnotized. You didn't even realize you were saying it." She said sounding more alert.

"Wait. What? I mean when?" I questioned angrily in disbelief.

"Back when you were twenty two. You did a hypnotherapy session. It lasted for 3 hours and the therapist never stopped it and brought you back into consciousness when she should have. As soon as you were free of the hypnosis you literally had a nervous beakdown. You stopped speaking for three days. The therapist had her assistant type up the session and sent me the report. I was there with you and honestly, it's been ten years now and I have yet to see anything like it and I have hypnotherapy sessions of my own with my patients. You weren't speaking as yourself. You sounded like a child with your same expanded vocabulary. It was creepy. You sounded like Franklin off of 'My Wife and Kids' but with a country accent. You were cussing but your voice still sounded childlike. It was the creepiest thing I ever witnessed Lilly. You were in the hospital for three days in the mental health ward. You wouldn't move, talk or eat for three days. I don't know what made you snap out of it. But when I came up to see you on the third day and you were back to your normal self you couldn't remember being hypnotized or anything you said. The therapists advised not to bring it up ever again. However, since you became my patient and after all our couch sessions just talking and delving deeper into your mind I knew you needed to know the truth. I felt this was the best way to tell you your story. I'm sorry. I really thought you were going to catch on awhile ago. The other therapist said it was best that I not force it to come to you but rather let it come to your memory all on its own. I was scared you would go into another nervous breakdown. Please forgive me. How are you feeling now?" She asked after her rambling although sounding genuinely concerned.

"Honestly, Mariee this is all a lot to take in. Part of me is happy, you know that I finally got some answers. But part of me is scared like how could I not remember that? I have to reread the book again now that I know I'm reading about myself. In a way I feel like I got some kind of closure because that book was actually making me do some crazy things."

"What do you mean?" She asked inquisitively.

"Oh nothing too serious. I just noticed I wasn't feeling myself." I lied.

"Well…ok…well now that you know what happened, I have something else to show you. Can you be at your office at nine tomorrow? It's important."

"Yeah I guess. I'm still low key mad at you." I said finally feeling somewhat at peace and making light of the situation.

"Yeah yeah. I know! But you woke me up. Can I go back to sleep now or nah?" She said laughing right along with me.

"Yeah I guess. Good night girl. See you in the morning." I said.

I hung up the phone. Poured me another glass of wine and started the shower. It was time for me to get ready for bed. I wondered what more Mariee had to show me. I thought as I drifted off to sleep in my California king bed curled up tightly in my purple comforter hugging a pillow for comfort as if it was my man.

# *Chapter Fifteen*

After dropping Stephanie off at school I drove to my office to meet with Mariee. I walked into my firm looking at the wooden plaque that read Lovejoy and Jones Psychology Center. I was proud of myself. After everything I went through I still came out on top. With everything I recently found out about myself, I never should have made it for real. But God….

"Hey boo!" Mariee greeted me with a hug.

"Hey love. I want to thank you so much! I'm just happy I have some information. You have no idea how it felt to know something so horrible happened to you and have no idea as to what actually happened. I thank God for you I just feel so relieved now." I said hugging her back extra tight.

"Awww! I'm so glad you said that. You had a girl nervous calling me in the middle of the night cussing like you done lost your damn mind." Mariee said laughing and hugging me tighter.

"Yeah. Yeah. Finding that out had me all messed up in the head. I was going crazy for real. SO what else you got for me?" I said to her eagerly.

"I can only imagine Lilly. Well, once you decided to become my patient you gave me full access to all your medical records. Remember that? " Mariee said digging in her file cabinet for what she wanted to show me.

"Ok, I don't have anything really crazy in my medical records except my Lupus and Fibromyalgia diagnosis. So what does that have to do with anything?" I asked confused as to where she was going with this.

"Nothing. But I went way back girl. You know I'm thorough. And….Well…I found a psych report from back when you were like 6 years old." Mariee said pulling out the papers and handing them to me.

I could feel her eyes piercing through my skin as she waited for me to look up from reading it. It was an 18 page report. I was only skimming through reading the highlighted lines.

## Assessment of Current Functions

Presenting Problems: Shanna was removed from the care of her mother Diane Bow in 1991 due to Ms. Bow's inability to care for and protect her. Ms. Bow has a significant substance abuse problem and has not sought treatment. Shanna and her siblings were found alone during a fire with Ms. Bow when she was too intoxicated to care for them. Shanna has also been sexually abused by her stepfather. Shanna's father is currently incarcerated and therefore not a placement option. Shanna historically had to assume the parental role in an attempt to provide the necessary daily living needs to maintain survival for she and her siblings. Although she initially resisted, she has since relinquished this role to her current foster mother. Shanna also presented with poor communication skills, had problems attaching to others as she would isolate herself whenever anyone got too close, sexually acted out on herself, exhibited eating disorder like behavior such as overeating and hoarding food, and problems with manipulation as a survival tactic, all of which have decreased to normalcy. Her overall sense of self, taking care of her own needs as opposed to others, and self esteem has notably improved. Shanna continues to have some difficulty with maladaptive manipulative behaviors. She has difficulty relating to peers and major trust issues.

Current Clinical Impressions: Shanna meets the criteria for Posttraumatic Stress Disorder, Chronic. Shanna has been sexually abused by her stepfather and she was helpless to prevent it. Symptoms that she currently is exhibiting include: recurrent recollection of the event as displayed by her frequent sexual acting out (according to the last foster home) diminished interest and participation in family activities, feelings of detachment or estrangement from others, restricted range of affect, difficulty falling asleep and irritability/anger issues.

Shanna had been in a series of foster placements that were disrupted due to abuse in the homes. She had learned in her short life that she could not trust the adults that surrounded her to stay in her life or to be there for her when she needed them. This apparent chaotic and unsafe lifestyle with her biological mother and last two previous foster placements resulted in Shanna's need to assume the caretaker role for her two younger brothers, feeding and diapering them, even babysitting for them alone. Her survival skills manifested into inappropriate ways to meet her needs, and she lacked the basic understanding that her needs are of equal value. It was also noted that her previous foster mother did not make much effort to curb Shanna nor her brother's sexually acting out behaviors because she was afraid it would "ruin their chances for adoption." There is also knowledge that another adolescent child in one of the foster homes sexually perpetuated on her and her brothers as well. As another one of her survival tactics she represses any bad memories because she's unable to handle them emotionally and needed to be strong for her brothers.

I stopped reading as tears rolled down my face. I looked up and Mariee had left me in her office to read my report in private. I'm glad she did. All I ever really wanted was the answers to my questions. I wanted to know what I repressed back into my mind so long ago and why I was having panic attacks after a sudden flashback of things that happened to me as a child. I would wake up in a hot sweat after having a bad nightmare, the obsessive compulsive habit of checking behind the shower curtain every time I go to the bathroom, and constantly isolating myself from others as an attempt to not get hurt if they do leave like everyone else did. It gave me answers as to why I am the way I am and hopefully the flashbacks will stop because now I know exactly what happened. I let out a sigh of relief, wiped my tears, and walked out of Mariee's office into my own so I can get my things.

"You alright Lilly?" Mariee asked peeking her head through the door.

"Yeah. Thank you so much. I need to take like a week off. I have way too much going on right now. Is that cool love?" I asked knowing she would understand.

"Of course. You know I got the security guard and Janay here. Just make sure she reschedules any

219

appointments you might have this week." Mariee said comfortingly.

"Okay, I will. I can't leave my kids hanging. By the way, I should tell you that I have adopted a daughter." I said to Mariee quickly sliding it in.

"Whaaaat?! When? I know that's been your dream since you were a child but you haven't mentioned it in awhile." Mariee exclaimed excitedly.

"Yeah, I've been working on it for awhile now but I didn't know if it was going to officially happen which is why I never said anything. You know how tedious that process is." I lied to Mariee again.

"Wow! That's awesome! I'm so happy for you!" Mariee exclaimed running up to me for another hug.

"Yeah I have to take the week off and get the house ready for her, get her enrolled in school, and just get to know her, you know?" I said.

"Yeah hun, I'm sure you do. Well you take your week off momma!" Mariee giggled finding humor in her calling me momma.

"Haha! I'm a sexy momma though." I said laughing with her as I walked out our center leaving her the only psychologist in the office for a week. I knew she could handle it. I was just glad that I was finally able to relax and enjoy life. I found peace through my pain.

# Chapter Sixteen

A week had passed and Stephanie and I were adjusting well with one another. We still had a court date ahead later on in the month to make it completely official but I was confident things were going to go as planned. I had only seen Khyail once this whole week and I missed him so much. I could tell he had some issues with me taking in Stephanie and didn't believe the story about her being my god daughter and that her parents died leaving me her only living guardian. He normally would come over every night but all this week he's been rather antisocial with me. However, I see him on facebook and instagram out and about having a blast. I guess he didn't like the fact that I had a child. He called me this morning saying he was coming to pick me up to take me out to eat. My aunt came and got Stephanie to take her to get her nails and hair done. I was just waiting for Khyail to show up. He picked me up in his black 2016 Dodge Charger and I got in. He wouldn't tell me where we were going and was acting like it was a big surprise. The first stop was at Marathon gas station. He got out and went inside to pay for gas. I looked over noticing his phone was still on the charger. I heard a voice telling me he's hiding something, go through it. No sooner did I hear that did I pick up the phone and was searching through texts as quickly as possible.

-You made me feel so special last night baby, thank you. You feel so good to me.

-Anytime baby, that pussy is fire.

I stopped reading seeing him come out the door walking towards the gas pump. I was sick to my stomach. I could feel the butterflies as my stomach knotted up and my heart began to race. I wanted to kill him. He got in the car.

"What's wrong with you?" He questioned seeing my dead facial expression.

"Nothing. We're going to have to go another time. I just got a bad migraine and I think I'm going to throw up."I said.

"Ok baby. You want me to stay with you?" He asked as if he really cared.

"No, go do whatever. I just want to be alone." I said trying my best to contain my anger.

"Ok ok…. I understand how your headaches can be. I'll take you back home."

No he didn't understand but he was about to see exactly how bad of a headache I can be. You would think he would be smarter than to betray a killer. We rode in silence the whole way home as I stared off into the clouds. We pulled up at my house and I got out and slammed the door. I seen him pick up his phone and speed off without even waiting to see if I made it inside my house. He had changed. He would have never of done that before. As I walked up to the door I noticed a book hanging out of my mail box. It had a post it on it that read:

*This is the second part of the session.*

*Love,*

*Mariee.*

The book was just like the other one, handwritten like a journal. I couldn't imagine what more there was to know but I knew I was going to end up reading it. Curiosity always got the best of me. I didn't know what to do about Khyail but I knew I needed a break from him before I have a psychotic break and kill him. I should have known he would choose something or someone over me like everyone else but it still hurt. The pain in my heart was undeniable. I don't normally stand for cheating but Khyail has something on me. And even more seriously, How do I know he won't tell the police on me if I make him mad? I can't believe he's cheating on me! I wondered how long it had been going on. Trust really is a fool's suicide, I thought as I walked into my house. I guess I would take this time to focus on Stephanie and I. Me and my daughter vs. everybody from now on. Trust issues on a thousand percent.

# *Afterward*

I chose to write this book for a multitude of reasons. I wanted to provide a light in an all too dark part of the foster care system involving child abuse and sexual abuse, to help other grown women who went through sexual abuse as a child, but mostly to heal myself through creative expression. When I started writing this book it was such a struggle because I wanted it to be completely factual, only my real life. I didn't want to take away from the authenticity of the story at all. However, my nerves started to get the best of me and I wondered what people would think of me if they knew this happened to me and I thought like this as a result. So my direction for the book began to change and I wanted to tell the story of what I would want to do to a child molester and from there the book became a lot easier to write because it was as if I was living out a dark fantasy of killing pedophiles. It was still always a struggle when it came to the parts of the book about my childhood but I pulled through. Those parts are very raw and vivid because I wanted full disclosure and authenticity when it came to the sexual abuse of a child. I wanted the story told exactly as I remembered it and I wanted my thoughts and feelings at that time to be properly conveyed and felt by the reader. As a child and growing up all the way until the age of twenty, I harbored such strong anger and resentment towards my biological mother because, well, I blamed her for everything. Thankfully before she passed I was able to talk to her and received much needed closure. People can only love from their level of understanding. Her childhood was ripped from her too and I realized she was just as broken as me. I just wish she was able to rid herself of the pain that haunted her before she passed. This is the first of a three part novel telling the truth of my childhood in this fictional story. Stay tuned for the next one!

All

Praises

Be

To

God.

www.ingramcontent.com/pod-product-compliance
Lightning Source LLC
Chambersburg PA
CBHW071020280326
41935CB00011B/1425